Headline Series

No. 306   FOREIGN POLICY ASSOCIATION   Spring

Divided Korea:
United Future?

by Bruce Cumings

Introduction 3

1   Legacies from the Past 7

2   Eclipse by Japan 15

3   Liberation, Two States and War 24

4   South Korean Politics 37

5   North Korean Politics 51

6   The Two Economies 63

7   Korea's Relationship to the World 76

   Talking It Over 85

   Annotated Reading List 87

Cover Design: Ed Bohon $5.95

The Author

BRUCE CUMINGS has followed Korean affairs since serving there in the Peace Corps in the late 1960s. He is a graduate of Denison University, with a Ph.D. in political science and East Asian history from Columbia University. He has taught at Swarthmore College, the University of Washington, the University of Chicago and Northwestern University where he is now John Evans Professor of International History and Politics; he also directs the Center for International and Comparative Studies.

His first volume of *The Origins of the Korean War* was cowinner of the Harry S. Truman Award in 1982 and won the John Fairbank Award of the American Historical Association in 1983. The second and concluding volume was published by Princeton University Press in 1990 and won the Quincy Wright Award from the International Studies Association.

The Foreign Policy Association

The Foreign Policy Association is a private, nonprofit, nonpartisan educational organization. Its purpose is to stimulate wider interest and more effective participation in, and greater understanding of, world affairs among American citizens. Among its activities is the continuous publication, dating from 1935, of the HEADLINE SERIES. The author is responsible for factual accuracy and for the views expressed. FPA itself takes no position on issues of U.S. foreign policy.

HEADLINE SERIES (ISSN 0017-8780) is published four times a year, Spring, Summer, Fall and Winter, by the Foreign Policy Association, Inc., 470 Park Avenue So., New York, N.Y. 10016. Chairman, Paul B. Ford; President, John Temple Swing; Editor in Chief, Nancy Hoepli-Phalon; Senior Editors, Ann R. Monjo and K.M. Rohan; Editorial Assistant, June Lee. Subscription rates, $20.00 for 4 issues; $35.00 for 8 issues; $50.00 for 12 issues. Single copy price $5.95; double issue $11.25. Discount 25% on 10 to 99 copies; 30% on 100 to 499; 35% on 500 and over. Payment must accompany all orders. Postage and handling: $2.50 for first copy; $.50 each additional copy. Second-class postage paid at New York, N.Y., and additional mailing offices. POSTMASTER: Send address changes to HEADLINE SERIES, Foreign Policy Association, 470 Park Avenue So., New York, N.Y. 10016. Copyright 1995 by Foreign Policy Association, Inc. Design by K.M. Rohan. Printed at Science Press, Ephrata, Pennsylvania. Spring 1994. Published June 1995.

Library of Congress Catalog Card No. 95-61187
ISBN 0-87124-164-1

Introduction

WHEN AMERICANS think of Korea, they think of a small country surrounded by larger powers—Korea as "a shrimp among whales," to take one image. Korea is roughly the size of Italy or England, with a total population today of over 68 million, almost equal to unified Germany. Korea is referred to as remote or far-off; the Japanese enjoy calling North Korea the remotest country. But Northeast Asia is only remote from the Eurocentric and civilizational standpoint of "the West," and North Korea is remote only because of the cold war and its studied policy of isolation and self-reliance. Both Koreas are also modern in the 1990s, yet no Westerner imagined a modern Korea in 1900, none predicted it in 1945, and experts still did not envision it just a generation ago. Instead, old Korea seemed lacking in everything that counted in the West: bustling commerce, empirical science, a stable middle class, a spirit of enterprise, innovative technology.

How then did they do it? Something must have been missed in Western observations of Korea before 1970. It might have been history that was overlooked. Consideration of Korea's long record of con-

The Foreign Policy Association gratefully acknowledges The Freeman Foundation's support for this issue of the HEADLINE SERIES.

tinuous existence and advanced civilization can lead to an understanding of one of the 20th century's most remarkable achievements, a modern Korea that now can produce almost anything the rest of the world can, and often do it better. Korea does not present the Westerner with a smooth narrative of progress toward industrial mastery, however. In 1910 it lost its centuries-old independence to Japan, and it remained an exploited colony until 1945. Then came national division, political turmoil, a devastating war and the death and dislocation of millions—which only left Korea still divided and in desperate poverty. A decade later South Korea began to industrialize and today its politics are democratic, but only after two military coups and several popular rebellions. North Korea developed more quickly after the war, but it soon reaped the diminishing returns of a political and economic system designed to remedy the problems of the 1930s, not those of the 1960s or 1990s. For several years many analysts have said that North Korea is on the verge of collapse, but it survives and the peninsula remains divided and subject to all the conflicts and passions that the rest of the world knew during the long years of the cold war.

More than a million soldiers still confront each other across a Korean "Mason-Dixon line," armed to the teeth with the latest equipment; the line is so firm that hardly anything crosses it, not even mail between divided families. Factor into this situation the great 20th-century divide between communism and capitalism, surround this country with four big powers, then add 37,000 young American soldiers, the latest fighter-bombers, a multitude of military bases and an array of naval forces, and the result might be a complete anachronism, given the end of the cold war on a world scale. Yet this is Korea today, having just emerged from a confrontation over nuclear weapons in the spring of 1994 that very nearly led to war between the United States and North Korea.

Because Korea remains a cold-war island (or peninsula) in a post-cold-war world, it is appropriate to remind readers of the continuing danger of war. But one does so at the risk of conjuring up an old, misleading image: Korea, the war-torn, helpless mendicant of the 1950s. The traveler to the two Koreas today could not imagine the devastation of 1953. In Seoul, the South Korean capital, the traveler is overwhelmed by the shimmering skyscrapers, the bustling citizenry, the raw dynamism of one of the world's most rapidly growing countries. Pyongyang, the North's capital, is a modern city, too, with wide boulevards, beautiful parks and a society of workaholics also devoted to economic development. Yet both Koreas grew on entirely different models, the South emphasizing exports, the North emphasizing self-reliance.

In politics there is another image: worst-case socialism meets worst-case capitalism. North Korea still remains a leading favorite for that society most resembling George Orwell's *1984,* and from 1961 through 1987 South Korea was a symbol of authoritarian politics and human-rights violations. Although South Korea has made important strides toward democracy since that time, it still lacks many of those attributes dear to the heart of Western liberalism.

1989 Alters Korea's Status

If these images have been fairly stable over recent years, it is also important to note that they may not hold for the near future. Korea's position in the international system, which was frozen into the cold war for nearly four decades, has changed dramatically since 1989. Russia and China now have extensive economic and diplomatic relations with the South, and both Moscow and Beijing have drastically reoriented their relations with the North. The United States and North Korea, meanwhile, made a watershed agreement in October 1994 that has led to the opening of modest diplomatic relations and growing trade, while promising to end the confrontation over North Korea's nuclear program. If the cold war ended in Europe only in 1989, it ended in most of East Asia with the conclusion of the Vietnam War and the warming of U.S.-China ties in the 1970s. In the 1990s Korea is joining an international environment that has changed dramatically: China and the United States are friends, China and Russia have extensive trade as do China and Taiwan; Japan has diplomatic relations with all the other big powers and trades widely with them, and it has economic relations with both Koreas (Japan being North Korea's main capitalist trading partner).

Still, it took a very long time for the changed external environment to effect corresponding changes internal to the Korean peninsula, and those that have occurred in the 1990s are still reversible. But it is now *unification?*

possible to hope that the cherished dream of all Koreans, a reunified nation, might soon be realized. How Koreans will reconcile their two different systems and finally reunify still remains a mystery for the future, but it is something all Koreans are thinking about as the millennium nears.

Of the various countries divided after World War II, Korea was first, in the ashes of Japan's defeat, and it will be united last. This itself is an injustice, but the greater injustice stems from the fact that Korea was not a belligerent in World War II and has never harmed its neighbors. In other words, Korea's experience differs sharply from that of Germany: the latter's unity is little more than a century old, and the territory of Germany was laced with ethnic and linguistic variation. So, it is *divided* Korea that is the anomaly, and therefore reconciliation and reunion have been and will remain the overriding goals of most Koreans.

It is particularly important and urgent for Americans to learn about, or deepen their knowledge of, the two Koreas. The United States has an enormous responsibility for the shape of the Korean peninsula today, a military role that could make it a belligerent overnight in any new war, and deep economic and political relationships with the Republic of Korea (ROK) in the South. If Americans fail to comprehend their past and present role in Korea, they do so at their peril, for Korea in the postwar period has had a knack for forcibly bringing itself to American attention.

1

Legacies from the Past

K OREA'S RECORDED HISTORY extends back before the birth of Christ, and its unitary existence dates from the seventh century A.D. It had many of the requisites of nationhood—political unity, common language, ethnic homogeneity, well-recognized international boundaries—long before the nations of Europe emerged. Indeed, Korea is one of the few nations in the world where ethnic and linguistic unity coincide exactly with national boundaries (Japan is another).

Like most other people, of course, contemporary Koreans in North and South think they have escaped history and tradition in the dizzying pace of an energetic 20th century. Meanwhile, they move in ways that would be inexplicable without reconnoitering a much longer period. Old Korea was a universe all its own, a fully realized human history like no other. It was a world defined by virtue, and if the virtues may be in retreat in contemporary Korea, as they are everywhere else, they still play upon Korean minds.

Today those virtues come under the catchall term, Confucianism. This is often said to be a conservative philosophy, stressing tradition,

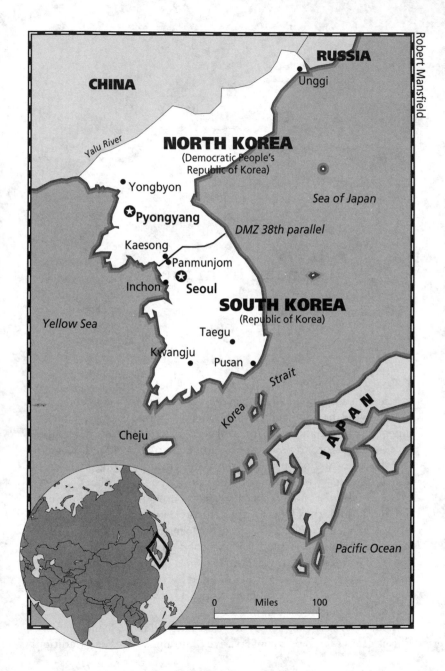

Robert Mansfield

CHINA

RUSSIA

Unggi

Yalu River

NORTH KOREA
(Democratic People's
Republic of Korea)

Yongbyon

★ Pyongyang

Sea of Japan

DMZ 38th parallel

Kaesong

Panmunjom

Inchon

★ Seoul

SOUTH KOREA
(Republic of Korea)

Yellow Sea

Taegu

Kwangju

Pusan

Korea Strait

JAPAN

Cheju

Pacific Ocean

0   Miles   100

veneration of a past golden age, careful attention to the performance of ritual, disdain for material things, obedience to superiors and a preference for relatively "frozen" social hierarchies. If Confucianism had those characteristics, it also had others—a salutary loyalty to one's family, for example, which might translate into competition with other families over material wealth; an emphasis on moral remonstrance, for another, that gives to students and scholars an ethical stance from which to speak truth to those in power. Much commentary on contemporary Korea focuses on the alleged authoritarian, antidemocratic character of this Confucian legacy. Yet one-sided emphasis on these aspects would never explain the extraordinary commercial bustle of South Korea, the materialism and conspicuous consumption of new elites, or the determined struggles for democratization put up by South Korean workers and students. At the same time, the assumption that North Korean communism broke completely with the past would blind one to continuing Confucian legacies there: its family-based politics, the succession to rule of the leader's son, and the extraordinary veneration of the state's founder, Kim Il Sung.

In 1392 the Yi Dynasty (also known as the Choson Dynasty) replaced the old Koryo Dynasty founded in 935 (from which comes the name Korea; South Korea calls itself Hanguk, a usage dating from the 1890s, while North Korea uses Choson to translate "Korea") and inaugurated a 500-year period of Confucian statecraft that did not end until 1910. By the late 19th century, Korea seemed so suffused with Confucian doctrine that foreign travelers termed it "more Confucian than China"; this was an exaggeration that overlooked the many innovations and differences in the Korean brand, but nonetheless the heritage has unquestionably stamped Korea as indelibly as it did China. It remains a powerful influence today.

Confucianism began with the family and an ideal model of relations between family members. It then generalized this family model to the state, and to an international system (the Chinese world order). The principle was hierarchy within a reciprocal web of duties and obligations: the son obeyed the father by following the dictates of filial piety; the father provided for and educated the son. Daughters obeyed mothers (and mothers-in-law!), younger siblings followed older siblings, wives were subordinate to husbands. The superior prestige and

9

privileges of older adults made longevity a prime virtue. Generalized to politics, a village followed the leadership of venerated elders, and citizens revered a king or emperor who was thought of as the father of the state. Extended to international affairs, the Chinese emperor was the big brother of the Korean king.

The glue holding the system together was education, meaning indoctrination into Confucian norms and virtues that began in early childhood with the reading of the Confucian classics. The model figure was the "true gentleman," the virtuous and learned scholar-official who was equally adept at poetry or statecraft. Even the poorest families would seek to spare one son from work in the fields so that he could study for exams that, if passed, would bring him an official position and, it was hoped, transform the situation of the rest of the family.

How long have Koreans taken education seriously? A Dutch sailor named Hendrik Hamel found himself beached quite unexpectedly on Korean shores in 1656 and later wrote that Koreans indulged in a "national devotion to education." Indeed, aristocrats and "free men" alike "take great care of the education of their children, and put them very young to learn to read and write, to which the nation is much addicted."

Until the 1890s Korean students had to master the extraordinarily difficult classical Chinese language, learning tens of thousands of written characters and their many meanings; rote memorization was the typical method. Throughout the Yi Dynasty all official records, all formal education, and most written discourse were in classical Chinese. The Chinese language so profoundly penetrated Korean culture that most Korean arts and literature used Chinese models right down through the last century.

Aristocrats, Scholar-Officials, Landlords, Commoners

A hierarchy of class and status is even older than Korea's Confucian heritage and it persists today in many ways—even in the Korean language, in which verb forms vary according to the status or age of the person to whom one is talking, and elders can only be addressed with elaborate honorifics. The Koryo Dynasty's composite elite forged a tradition of aristocratic continuity that lasted down to the modern era. This elite fused aristocratic privilege and political power through marriage alliances and control of land and central political office, and it fortified this class position to the point of impregnability by making it hereditary. Koryo established a social pattern in which a landed gentry mixed its control of property with a Confucian- or Buddhist-educated stratum of scholar-officials, usually residing in the capital; often scholars and landlords were one and the same person, but in any case landed wealth and bureaucratic position were powerfully fused. At the center there emerged a strong bureaucracy influenced by Confucian statecraft that sought to influence local power and militated against the Japanese or European feudal pattern of castle towns, landed domains and parceled sovereignty backed by a strong military class. (Korea had no military tradition comparable to Japan's samurai, or warlord aristocracy, although Koreans revere military leaders who have defeated foreign invasions—such as Yi Sun-shin, whose armor-clad "turtle" ships and sophisticated naval warfare helped hold off the Japanese during invasions in the 1590s.)

Buddhism coexisted with Confucianism throughout the Koryo period, richly influencing daily life and perhaps bequeathing to modern Korea its characteristic eclectic religious belief: Koreans are often Confucians, Buddhists and Christians at the same time. Nor was Koryo Buddhism only of the other worldly variety: many monks got rich from commerce, agriculture, animal husbandry, wine-making and loans made at high interest; furthermore it was a state religion, merging philosophy with political power. And finally, during the Koryo and later periods, these were fighting monks: monkish guerrillas helped turn back Japanese invasions.

The new elite that came to power in 1392 was more or less the old elite, but they did accomplish a thorough renovation of the existing society. Much of what is now called Korean culture or Korean tradition was the result of a major social reorganization accomplished by self-conscious Confucian ideologues in the fifteenth century. What started as a military putsch by General Yi Song-gye in 1392 ended up in the apparent solidifying of a hierarchical Confucian society much like the one Westerners first encountered many centuries later. An unquestionable effect of the many new laws, if not their clear intent, was a radical diminution of the social position of women and an expropriation of women's property.

Most of the Yi Dynasty elite came from a relative handful of prominent families, tracing their line back to a prominent male. The top families were the *yangban*, literally meaning the two ranks (military and civilian) that staffed the Yi Dynasty, but designating a potent aristocratic fusion of landed wealth and political power. Unlike the Chinese models, elite status was hereditary: one had to demonstrate that at least one ancestor in the previous four generations had been a yangban. To be a "distinguished ancestor" it was good to be a landowner, an official, and above all a scholar. Best of all was to wrap all three together in one person or family. Running close behind was the virtue of marrying well, that is, finding a daughter from another prominent family. Those at the top thus stitched a web of property, status and lineage that was well nigh impenetrable from below through much of the dynasty.

Although merchants ranked higher than the low-born classes, Confucian elites frowned on commercial activity and squelched it as much as possible right down to the twentieth century. Even in the late nineteenth century there were no large commercial cities in Korea, and no commercial class worthy of the name (which is not to say there were no merchants). Peasants ranked higher than merchants because they worked the life-giving land, but the life of the peasantry was almost always difficult during the dynasty. The low-born classes were probably worse off than peasant farmers, however, given very high rates of slavery for much of the Yi period.

Stability, Persistence and China's Benign Neglect

Yi Dynasty Confucian doctrines of hierarchy did not stop at the water's edge, but also informed a foreign policy known as serving the great, the great being China—and not just China, but China of the Ming Dynasty. Korea was China's little brother, a model tributary state, and in many ways the most important of China's allies.

The central government's ultimate weakness was its inability to extract resources effectively—primarily because of aristocratic power. What James B. Palais, the premier historian of the Yi Dynasty, called a "fusion of aristocratic status with private landownership" constituted "an amalgam that was almost as resistant to the fiscal encroachments of the central government as a bona fide feudal nobility."

With Korea's opening to the West and Japan in 1876, the Yi Dynasty faltered and then collapsed in a few decades. How, therefore, can one account for its five-century longevity, which included devastating invasions by the Japanese and the Manchus? In essence, the traditional system was adaptable, even supple, although in the end it could not withstand the full foreign onslaught of technically advanced imperial powers with strong armies. The old agrarian bureaucracy managed the interplay of different and competing interests by a system of checks and balances. The king and the bureaucracy kept watch on each other, the royal clans watched both, scholars could criticize ("remonstrate") from the moral position of Confucian doctrine, secret inspectors and censors went around the country to watch for rebellion and assure accurate reporting, landed aristocrats sent sons into the bureaucracy to protect family interests and local potentates influenced the county magistrates sent down from the central administration. The centralized facade masked a dispersal of power, sets of competing interests, and institutional checks and balances that prevented one group from getting all that there was to get. The Yi Dynasty was not a system that modern Koreans would wish to restore or live under, but in its time it was a sophisticated political system, adaptable enough and persistent enough to give unified rule to Korea for half a millennium.

Many legacies of this agrarian-bureaucratic system persist in Korea today. In the South, county leaders are moved very frequently from post to post so that they do not become too responsive to local concerns and forget the central government. In the North, those at the top frequently castigate the "bureaucratism" of officials who put on airs, send inadequate or false reports to the capital, or fail both to remember the policies of the central government and the necessity to adapt them to differing local situations. Kim Il Sung was even known to have sent secret inspectors to watch local bureaucratic performance. Both Koreas also know how to preserve central power. Kim effectively passed on power to his son, Kim Jong Il; Park Chung Hee ruled for 18 years against much opposition, and was only removed by an assassin; Chun Doo Hwan's tenure ended amid massive urban protest and demands for free elections, yet he succeeded in passing the mantle on to his friend and confidant, Roh Tae Woo.

Korean states have always had to work out their fate while thinking about the often stronger powers that surround the peninsula. Claiming to have been invaded more than 900 times (an exaggeration), Koreans for good reason have tended to view foreign powers as predatory and up to no good.

As a small power, Korea had to learn to be shrewd in foreign policy, and it had a good example of that in China. Koreans cultivated the sophisticated art of "low-determines-high" diplomacy, seeking to use foreign power for their own ends, wagging the dog with its tail. Thus the two Koreas strike foreign observers as rather dependent on big power support, yet both not only claim but strongly assert their absolute autonomy and independence as nation-states, and both are adept at manipulating their big-power clients. North Korea may have a bizarre and heavy-handed internal system, but until the mid-1980s it was masterful in maneuvering between the two Communist giants to get something from each and to prevent either from dominating the North; in the 1990s its shrewd diplomacy got much from the United States, in spite of the North's deeply threatened status.

The soft spot that Koreans have in their hearts for China should not blind anyone to the main characteristic of Korea's traditional diplomacy: isolationism, even what historian Dr. Kim Key-Hiuk has called exclusionism. For 300 years after the Japanese invasions of the 1590s, Korea isolated itself from Japan, dealt harshly with errant Westerners washing up on its shores, and after the Manchu conquest in 1644, also kept the Chinese at arm's length. Thus Westerners called Korea the Hermit Kingdom, expressing the pronounced streak of obstinate hostility toward foreign power and the deep desire for independence that marked traditional Korea. Ethnocentric and obnoxious to foreigners, a self-contained, autonomous Korea not besmirched by things foreign remains an ideal for many Koreans. North Korea has exercised a Hermit Kingdom option by remaining one of the more isolated states in the world, and it is really South Korea that, since 1960, has been revolutionary in the Korean context by pursuing an open-door policy toward the world market and seeking a multilateral, varied diplomacy. Calls for self-reliance and expelling foreign influence will always get a hearing in Korea; this is one of its most persistent foreign policy traits.

2

Eclipse by Japan

EAST ASIA was "opened" by Western imperialism in about three decades. China was the first to succumb, during the Opium Wars of 1839–42; Japan came next when Commodore Matthew Perry's "black ships" appeared in Tokyo Bay in 1854; Korea was last, not because it was stronger, but perhaps because it was more recalcitrant. It did not sign its first international treaty until 1876, which was with Japan, not a Western power. Korea's descent into the maelstrom of imperial rivalry was quick after that, however, as Japan imposed a Western-style unequal treaty, giving its nationals extraterritorial legal rights and opening several Korean ports to international commerce.

So far little has been said about Korea's most numerous class, the millions of peasants who tilled the fields day in and day out so that the aristocracy could be free to conduct its pursuits, high-minded and otherwise. But these were the people who truly resisted imperial encroachment. After decades of agricultural distress, a movement arose in the 1860s under the name Eastern Learning. Its slogan: "Drive out the Japanese dwarfs and the Western barbarians, and praise righteousness." A combination of this internal rebellion and the Sino-Japanese War fought over Korea in 1894–95 spelled the end of Korean autonomy. For the next 10 years the Korean court was a shuttlecock batted around by the great powers.

In 1905 Japan emerged victorious. Capping decades of imperial rivalry in Northeast Asia, it defeated Russia in war and established a protectorate over Korea. U.S. President Theodore Roosevelt aided in the negotiations that brought this result, and Washington did not thereafter challenge Japanese control of Korea. Japan completed its seizure by annexing Korea in 1910 and putting an end to the Yi Dynasty. Korea only escaped the Japanese grip in 1945, when Japan lay prostrate under the American and Russian onslaught that brought World War II to a close.

This colonial experience was intense and bitter, and it shaped postwar Korea deeply. It led to both development and underdevelopment, agrarian growth and increased tenancy, industrialization and extraordinary dislocation, political mobilization and deactivation; it spawned a new role for the central state, new sets of Korean political leaders, communism and nationalism, armed resistance and treacherous collaboration; above all it left deep fissures and conflicts that have gnawed at the Korean national identity ever since.

Colonialism is often thought to have created new nations where none existed before by drawing national boundaries, bringing diverse tribes and peoples together, tutoring the natives in self-government, and preparing for the day when the imperial power decides to grant independence. But all of this existed in Korea for centuries before 1910.

By the turn of the century some Westerners marked the important changes that Korea's early attempts at reform and modernization had wrought; their views help Americans to understand the common Korean judgment that Japanese colonialism did nothing for Korea except to retard a progressive drive already well under way before 1910. Angus Hamilton, an American writing in 1904, found Korea to be "a land of exceptional beauty" and thought Seoul was much superior to Beijing. Seoul was the first city in East Asia to have electricity, trolley cars, a water system, telephone and telegraph all at the same time. Most of these systems were installed and run by Americans: the Seoul Electric Light Company, the Seoul Electric Car Company and the Seoul

"Fresh Spring" Water Company were all American firms. Hamilton described Seoul in this way:

> The streets are magnificent, spacious, clean, admirably made and well-drained. The narrow, dirty lanes have been widened; gutters have been covered, and roadways broadened.... Seoul is within measurable distance of becoming the highest, most interesting, and cleanest city in the East.

There was for him "no question of the superiority" of Korean living conditions, both urban and rural, to those in China (if not Japan). Schools of every description abounded in Seoul—law, engineering, medicine; he noted that King Kojong wanted personally to supervise all public business.

Thus the Japanese engaged not in creation, but in *substitution* after 1910: substituting a Japanese ruling elite for the Korean yangban scholar-officials, Japanese modern education for Confucian classics, Japanese capital and expertise for the incipient Korean versions, imperial coordination for the traditional bureaucracy, Japanese talent for Korean talent, and eventually even the Japanese language for Korean. Koreans never thanked the Japanese for these substitutions, did not credit Japan with creations, and instead saw Japan as snatching away the ancien régime, Korea's sovereignty and independence, its indigenous if incipient modernization, and above all its national dignity. Unlike some other colonial peoples, therefore, Koreans never saw Japanese rule as anything but illegitimate and humiliating. Furthermore, the very closeness of the two nations—in geography, in shared Chinese cultural influences, indeed in levels of development until the nineteenth century—made Japanese dominance all the more galling to Koreans and gave a peculiar intensity to the relationship, a love/hate dynamic that suggested to Koreans, "there but for accidents of history go we."

Bureaucratic Authoritarianism

Japan held Korea tightly, watched it closely and pursued an organized colonialism in which the planner and administrator, not a swashbuckling conqueror, was the model. The strong, highly centralized colonial state mimicked the role that the Japanese state had come to play in Japan—intervening in the economy, creating markets, spawning new industries, suppressing dissent. The Japanese built bureaucracies in Korea, all of them centralized and all of them big by colonial standards. Unlike, say, the relatively small British colonial cadre in India, the Japanese came in large numbers (700,000 by the 1940s), and the majority of colonizers worked in government service. For the first time in history, Korea had a national police, responsive to the central government, with its own communication and transportation facilities. The Japanese unquestionably strengthened central bureaucratic power in Korea, demolishing the old balance and tension with the landed aristocracy. Operating from the top down, they effectively penetrated below the county level and into the villages for the first time, and in some ways neither post-colonial Korean state has ever gotten over it: Korea is still a country with remarkably little local autonomy.

The huge Oriental Development Company organized and funded industrial and agricultural projects, and it came to own more than 20 percent of Korea's arable land; it employed an army of officials who fanned out through the countryside to supervise agricultural production. The official Bank of Korea performed central banking functions and provided credit to firms and entrepreneurs—almost all of them, of course, Japanese. Central judicial bodies wrote new laws establishing an extensive, "legalized" system of racial discrimination against Koreans, making them second-class citizens in their own country. Bureaucratic departments proliferated at the Government-General headquarters in Seoul, turning it into the nerve center of the country. Semi-official companies and conglomerates, including the big *zaibatsu* (Japanese cartels) such as Mitsubishi and Mitsui, laid railways, built ports, installed modern factories and, in short, remade the face of old Korea.

Politically, Koreans could barely breathe, but economically there was substantial, if unevenly distributed, growth—especially when compared to other colonies. Agricultural output rose substantially in the 1920s, and a "hothouse industrialization" took place in the 1930s. Growth rates in the Korean economy often outstripped those in Japan itself; recent research has indicated an annual growth rate for Korea of 3.6 percent in the period 1911–38, a rate of 3.4 percent for Japan itself. Koreans have always thought the benefits of this growth went entirely to Japan and that Korea would have developed rapidly without Japanese help. Nonetheless, the strong colonial state, the multiplicity of bureaucracies, the policy of administrative guidance for the economy, the use of the state to found new industries and the repression of labor unions and dissidents that always went with it provided a surreptitious model for both Koreas after World War II. Japan showed them an early version of the "bureaucratic-authoritarian" path to industrialization, and it was a lesson that seemed well-learned by the 1970s.

Political Division

The colonial period brought forth an entirely new set of Korean political leaders, spawned both by the resistance to and the opportunities of Japanese colonialism. The emergence of nationalist and Communist groups dates back to the 1920s; it is really in this period that the left-right splits of postwar Korea began. The transformation of the yangban aristocracy also began then. In the 1930s new groups of armed resisters, bureaucrats and (for the first time) military leaders emerged. Both North and South Korea remain profoundly influenced by political elites and political conflicts generated during colonial rule.

One legacy of the Yi Dynasty that the Japanese changed but did not destroy was the yangban aristocracy. The higher scholar-officials who did not leave on their own were pensioned off and replaced by Japanese, but many landlords were allowed to retain their holdings and encouraged to continue disciplining peasants and extracting rice. The traditional landholding system was put on a new legal basis, but tenancy continued and became more entrenched throughout the colonial period; by 1945 Korea had an agricultural tenancy system with few parallels in the world. More-traditional landlords were content to sit back and let Japanese officials increase output (by 1945 such people were widely viewed as treacherous collaborators with the Japanese), and strong demands emerged to have them share their land with the tenants. During the 1920s, however, another trend began as landlords became entrepreneurs.

The more-enlightened and entrepreneurial landlords were able to diversify their wealth, investing in industries (often textiles), banks, newspapers and schools. A good example would be "the Kochang Kims," a prominent family that owned the largest Korean textile mill,

19

founded what is now Korea University, and owned the leading Korean-language newspaper. Much of this activity was justified as the creation of Korean "national capital" and as a form of moderate nationalism and resistance to the Japanese. This group has been the source of much of the political leadership in postwar South Korea; Kim Song-su and his associates founded and led the Korean Democratic party after 1945, provided many officials during the American occupation (1945–48), and structured the moderate opposition to the governments of Syngman Rhee (1948–60) and Park Chung Hee (1961–79).

Resistance

Beginning on March 1, 1919, nationwide independence demonstrations shook Japanese colonialism to its roots; they were put down only with fierce repression. The year 1919 was a watershed for imperial rule in Korea: the leaders of the March 1 movement were moderate intellectuals and students who sought independence through nonviolent means and support from progressive elements in the West—especially U.S. President Woodrow Wilson (1913–21), whose famous Fourteen Points address included a strong call for self-determination for small nations. Their courageous witness and the nationwide demonstrations that they provoked remain a touchstone of Korean nationalism today. The movement succeeded in provoking reforms in Japanese administration, but its failure to realize independence also stimulated radical forms of anticolonial resistance.

Some Korean militants went into exile in China and the U.S.S.R. and founded early Communist and nationalist resistance groups. A Korean Communist party (KCP) was founded in Korea in 1925; a man named Pak Hon-yong was one of the organizers, and he became a leader of Korean communism in the South after 1945. Various nationalist groups also emerged during this period, including the exiled Korean Provisional Government (KPG) in Shanghai, which included future president Rhee among its members. Meanwhile a new policy of Japanese reformism spawned a moderate, gradualist tendency toward independence within Korea itself, while more radical labor and peasant organizations proliferated.

Sharp police repression and internal factionalism often made it impossible for radical groups to survive. Many nationalist and Communist leaders were thrown in jail in the early 1930s, only to emerge in 1945. When Japan invaded and then annexed Manchuria in 1931, however, a strong guerrilla resistance including Chinese and Koreans emerged. There may have been as many as 200,000 guerrillas (loosely connected, and including bandits and secret societies) fighting the Japanese in the early 1930s. After effective counterinsurgency campaigns the numbers declined to a few thousand by the mid-1930s. It was in this milieu that Kim Il Sung (originally named Kim Song-ju) and much of the later North Korean leadership emerged. Kim was a significant guerrilla leader by the mid-1930s, considered to be effective and dangerous by the Japanese. They formed a special counterinsurgent unit to track Kim down, and put Koreans in it as part of their divide-and-rule tactics.

This experience is important for understanding postwar Korea: the resistance to the Japanese is the main legitimating doctrine of the Democratic People's Republic of Korea (DPRK); the North Koreans trace the origin of the army, the leadership and their ideology back to that period. The top North Korean leadership was dominated from 1945 into the 1990s by a core group that fought the Japanese in Manchuria.

Japan attacked China in 1937 and the United States in 1941, and as this war took on global dimensions, Koreans for the first time had military careers opened to them. Although most were conscripted foot soldiers, a small number achieved officer status and a few even attained high rank. Virtually the entire officer corps of the ROK army during the Rhee period was drawn from Koreans with experience in the Japanese army. Lower-ranking officers also became prominent during the Park Chung Hee period, including Park himself, who had been a lieutenant in the Japanese army; Kang Young Hoon, the prime minister in the early years of the Roh Tae Woo government (1988–92), was also a veteran of this army. At least in part, the Korean War involved Japanese-trained military officers fighting Japanese-spawned resistance leaders.

Japan's far-flung war effort also caused a labor shortage throughout the empire. In Korea this meant that bureaucratic positions were more available to Koreans than at any previous time; thus a substantial cadre of Koreans got experience in government, local administration, police and judicial work, economic-planning agencies, banks and the like. That this occurred in the last decade of colonialism created a divisive legacy, however, for this was also the harshest period of Japanese rule, the time Koreans remember with greatest bitterness. Korean culture was quashed, and Koreans were required to speak Japanese and to take Japanese names. The majority suffered badly at the precise time that a minority was doing well. This minority acquired the taint of collaboration and never successfully shed it. Korea from 1937 to 1945 was much like Vichy France in the early 1940s: bitter experiences and memories continued to divide people, even within the same family; it was too painful to confront directly, and so for many years it amounted to buried history. Since the mid-1980s, however, historians in both Korea and Japan have begun to probe into this dark period, and courageous survivors have come forward to document the darkest episode, the forced and state-sponsored mobilization of between 100,000 and 200,000 Korean women as sexual slaves for the Japanese army.

Economic Development

In the mid-1930s, Japan entered a phase of heavy industrialization that embraced all of Northeast Asia. Unlike most colonial powers, Japan located heavy industry in its colonies, taking the means of production to the labor and raw materials. Manchuria and northern Korea got steel mills, auto plants, petrochemical complexes, enormous hydroelectric facilities; the region was held exclusively by Japan and tied to the home market to the degree that national boundaries became less important than the new transnational integrated production. To facilitate this production, Japan also built railroads, highways, cities, ports and other modern transportation and communication facilities. Some economists spoke of a "Korean boom" in the late 1930s, and by 1945 Korea proportionally had more road and railroad miles than any other Asian country except Japan, leaving only remote parts untouched by modern means of conveyance. These changes had been externally induced and served Japanese, not Korean, interests. Thus they represented a kind of overdevelopment.

The same changes contributed to underdevelopment in Korean society as a whole. Since the changes were not indigenous, the Korean upper and managerial classes did not flourish; instead their development was retarded, or ballooned suddenly at Japanese behest. Among the majority peasant class, change accelerated. Koreans became the mobile human capital used to work the new factories in northern Korea and Manchuria, mines and other enterprises in Japan, and urban factories in southern Korea. Between 1935 and 1945 Korea began its industrial revolution, with many of the usual characteristics: uprooting of peasants from the land, the emergence of a working class, urbanization and population mobility. In Korea the process was telescoped, giving rise to remarkable population movements. By 1945 about 11 percent of the entire Korean population was abroad (mostly in Japan and Manchuria), and fully 20 percent of all Koreans were either abroad or in a province other than that in which they were born (with most of the interprovincial movement resulting from southern peasants moving into northern industry). This was, by and large, a forced or mobilized movement; by 1942 it even included conscripted labor. Peasants lost land or rights to work land only to end up working in unfamiliar factory settings for a pittance.

When the colonial system abruptly terminated in 1945, millions of Koreans sought to return to their native villages from these far-flung mobilization details. But they were no longer the same people: they had grievances against those who remained secure at home, they had suffered material and status losses, they had often come into contact with new ideologies and they had all seen a broader world beyond the villages. It was this pressure cooker of a final decade that loosed upon postwar Korea a mass of changed and disgruntled people who created deep disorder in the liberation period and in the plans of the Americans and the Soviets.

3

Liberation, Two States and War

THE DECADE from 1943 to 1953 was the crucible of the national division and rival regimes that remain in Korea today. Nothing about the politics of contemporary Korea can be understood without comprehending the events of that decade. It was the breeding ground of the two Koreas, of a catastrophic war and of a reordering of international politics in Northeast Asia. In these events the United States had a major role, in many ways the predominant role among the big powers, and yet for most Americans and for many histories of the period, U.S. involvement in Korea was a footnote until war came in 1950. But Americans played the key role in dividing Korea and, with the Soviets, in jointly subjecting Korea to military occupation. This came as Japan's East Asian empire fell to the ground and Koreans tasted the joys of liberation.

Division and Occupation

There was no historical justification for Korea's division. There was no internal pretext for division, either: the 38th parallel was a line never noticed by the people of, say, Kaesong, the Koryo capital which the parallel cut in half. And then it became the only line that mattered to Koreans, a boundary to be removed by any means necessary. The political and ideological divisions associated with the cold war were the reasons for Korea's division.

In the days just before Koreans heard the voice of Emperor Hirohito broadcasting Japan's surrender and Korea's liberation on August 15, 1945, John J. McCloy of the State-War-Navy Coordinating Committee (SWNCC) directed two young colonels, Dean Rusk and Charles H. Bonesteel, to withdraw to an adjoining room and find a place to divide Korea. It was around midnight on August 10, the two atomic bombs had been dropped, the Soviet Red Army had entered the Pacific War, and American planners were rushing to arrange the Japanese surrender throughout the region. Given 30 minutes to do so, Rusk and Bonesteel looked at a map and chose the 38th parallel because it "would place the capital city in the American zone." Although the line was "further north than could be realistically reached ... in the event of Soviet disagreement," the Soviets made no objections—which "somewhat surprised" Rusk (whose subsequent account we rely on here). General Douglas MacArthur, the hero of the Pacific campaigns, issued General Order Number One for the Japanese surrender on August 15, including in it (and thus making public) the 38th-parallel decision. The Russians accepted in silence this division into spheres, while demanding a Russian occupation of the northern part of Hokkaido in Japan (which MacArthur refused).

American officials consulted no Koreans in coming to this decision, nor did they ask the opinions of the British or the Chinese, both of whom were to take part in a planned "trusteeship" for Korea—the decision was unilateral and hasty. Still, it grew out of previous American planning. The United States had taken the initiative in big-power deliberations on Korea during World War II, suggesting a multilateral trusteeship for postwar Korea to the British in March 1943, and to the Soviets at the end of the same year. President Franklin D. Roosevelt, worried about the disposition of enemy-held colonial territories and aware of colonial demands for independence, sought a gradualist policy of preparing colonials (like the Koreans) for self-government and independence. He knew that since Korea touched the Soviet border, the Russians would want to be involved in determining its fate. He hoped to get a Soviet commitment to a multilateral administration, to forestall unilateral solutions and provide an entry for American interests in Korea. Korean independence would only come at an appropriate time, or "in due course"—a phrase used in the 1943 Declaration of the Cairo Conference (where Roosevelt had met with Winston Churchill and Joseph Stalin). Stalin made no commitments to this policy, either, but seemed to enjoy watching Roosevelt and Churchill wrangle over the future of empire in the postwar world.

Roosevelt rarely consulted the State Department, but its planners began worrying as early as 1942, within months of Pearl Harbor, about the implications for Pacific security of Soviet involvement in Korea and questioned whether a trusteeship would give the United States enough influence in Korean affairs. They feared that the Soviets would bring with them Korean guerrillas who had been fighting the Japanese in Manchuria, the numbers of whom they grossly exaggerated (to as many as 30,000). Fearing that a trusteeship would not work, various planners began to develop ideas for a full military occupation that would assure a predominant American voice in postwar Korean affairs.

U.S. Policy Changes

This thinking was utterly new. No previous Administration had had the slightest interest in American involvement in Korean affairs, and Congress and the American people knew nothing about the proposed commitments. The 38th-parallel decision also reflected the absence of Roosevelt's experienced hand (he had died in April 1945). His idea had been to involve the Russians in a joint administration of Korea, to engage them and their interests in a country that touched their borders, thus giving them something while containing their ambitions. Partition was a much cruder device, abjuring diplomacy and simply drawing a line in the dirt; and from that point onward, no international diplomacy worked to solve an important Korean problem until the U.S.-DPRK nuclear agreement in October 1994. A diplomat named William W. Rockhill wrote at the turn of the century, "Korea is the place … there you will see diplomacy in the raw, diplomacy without gloves, perfume, or phrases." It was the same in 1945.

The policy was first to occupy Korea and then see if a trusteeship might be worked out with the Russians, British and Chinese. The United States gained Soviet adherence to a modified version of the trusteeship idea at the Foreign Ministers' Conference in December 1945, an important agreement that eliminated irrelevant British and Chinese influence, while suggesting that the two powers might ultimately come to terms on how to reunify Korea. This agreement also shortened the period of great-power involvement in Korean affairs to no more than five years, and it called for a provisional government to be set up. But even by that early date the agreement was too late, because the de facto policies of the two occupations had identified the Soviets with Kim Il Sung and various local people's committees, while the Americans backed Syngman Rhee and opposed the committees and widespread Korean demands for a thorough reform of colonial legacies.

In early 1947 officials in Washington grabbed control of Korean policy away from the occupation, however, when they decided to revive Japanese heavy industry and end the purges of wartime leaders, a policy long known as the "reverse course." This change was part and parcel of the development of the Truman Doctrine, which inaugurated "containment," and South Korea's potential importance to a revived Japan now gave the United States a strong reason to resist communism in Korea. Secretary of State George C. Marshall scribbled a note to Dean Acheson in late January 1947 that said, "Please have plan drafted of policy to organize a definite government of So. Korea and *connect up* [sic] its economy with that of Japan," a stunning mouthful.

This was the basic policy that governed the creation of the Republic of Korea in August 1948 and the end of the U.S. occupation. After the ROK was inaugurated, the Truman Administration replaced the military government with a 500-man Korean Military Advisory Group (KMAG), established an aid mission (known as the Economic Cooperation Administration, or ECA), pushed big aid bills through Congress to get the Korean economy moving and to equip an army capable of defending South Korea, and arranged for KMAG to retain operational control of the Korean police and military as long as American combat troops remained.

When the Korean War erupted, American policy changed once again. Had the United States simply sought to contain the Communist thrust into South Korea in the summer of 1950, it would have restored the 38th parallel as the dividing line between North and South when it crushed the North Korean army. Instead, American forces under General MacArthur marched into North Korea and sought to destroy the northern regime and unify the peninsula under Syngman Rhee's rule. Again, declassified documentation now shows that this action reflected a change from containment to a new policy, rollback. As policy planners described it, the United States for the first time had the chance to displace and transform some Communist real estate.

This American thrust, however, brought Chinese forces in on the northern side; these "volunteers" and a reinvigorated North Korean army pushed U.S. and South Korean forces out of the North within a month and caused a crisis in American domestic politics as backers of Truman fought with backers of MacArthur over the Administration's unwillingness to carry the war to mainland China. Although the war lasted another two years, until the summer of 1953, the outcome of early 1951 was definitive: a stalemate, and an American commitment to containment that accepted the de facto reality of two Koreas—and that explains why U.S. troops remain in South Korea today.

Soviet Policy

From the time of the czars, Korea has been a concern of Russian security. The Russo-Japanese War of 1904–05 was fought in part over the disposition of the Korean peninsula. It has often been thought that the Russians saw Korea as a gateway to the Pacific and especially to warmwater ports. Furthermore, Korea had one of Asia's oldest Communist movements. Thus it would appear that postwar Korea was of great concern to the Soviet Union and that its policy was a simple matter of Sovietizing northern Korea, setting up a puppet state, and then directing Kim Il Sung to unify Korea by force in 1950.

Now that Soviet archives have been partially opened, what Stalin really sought to do in Korea is better understood. First, the Soviets did not get a warmwater port out of their involvement in Korea. Second, they did not have an effective relationship with Korean Communists. Stalin purged and even shot many of the Koreans who had functioned in the Communist International; he gave little help to Kim Il Sung and other guerrillas in their struggle against the Japanese until after Pearl

Harbor. Original research by a Japanese scholar, Haruki Wada, has shown that from 1941 to 1945, Kim Il Sung and other Korean and Chinese guerrillas were given sanctuary in Sino-Russian border towns near Khabarovsk, trained at a small school, and dispatched as agents into Japanese-held territory. When the Soviets occupied Korea north of the 38th parallel in August 1945, they brought these Koreans (often termed Soviet-Koreans, even though most of them were not Soviet citizens) with them. Kim Il Sung, according to Wada, was chosen to lead the guerrilla group not by the Russians but by other Korean guerrilla leaders like Choe Hyon and Choe Yong-gon, both of whom later became prominent in the leadership. From August 1945 until February 1946 the Soviets worked with a coalition of Communists and nationalists, the latter led by a Christian educator named Cho Man-sik. They did not set up a central administration, nor did they create an army, unlike the Americans in the South; they also signed diplomatic agreements with the United States on trusteeship. Soviet power at that time in the Far East was flexible and resulted in the withdrawal of Soviet forces from Manchuria in early 1946.

In 1946 Soviet policy changed. In February an Interim People's Committee led by Kim Il Sung became the first central government in North Korea; in March a revolutionary land reform dispossessed landlords without compensation; in August a powerful political party (called the Korean Workers' party) came to dominate politics; and in the fall the first rudiments of a northern army appeared. Powerful central agencies nationalized major industries (they had of course mostly been owned by the Japanese) and began a two-year economic program on the Soviet model, with priority given to heavy industry. Nationalists and Christian leaders were denied all but pro forma participation in politics, and Cho Man-sik was held under house arrest. Kim Il Sung and his allies dominated the press, eliminating newspapers that contained opposition sentiments.

It was in the period 1946–48 that Soviet domination of North Korea was at its height, but at the end of 1948 the Soviets decided to withdraw their occupation troops from North Korea, signaling changes. This decision contrasted sharply with Soviet policies in Eastern Europe, where in some countries such as the former East Germany well over 300,000 Soviet troops remained until the Berlin Wall fell in 1989.

But no Soviet troops were again stationed in Korea. At the same time, tens of thousands of Korean soldiers who had fought in the Chinese civil war filtered back to Korea. This little-known but terribly important episode gave North Korea a formidable weapon in the civil struggle with the South; all through 1949 tough, crack troops with Chinese, not Soviet, experience returned to be integrated with the Korean People's Army (KPA, formally established in February 1948).

The Soviets kept advisers in the Korean government and military and they continued to trade and ship weaponry to North Korea. But without military force on hand and facing tough customers like Chinese leader Mao Zedong and Kim Il Sung, they were forced to compete with China for influence. So 1949 was a watershed year, the time when North Korea got some room to maneuver between Moscow and Beijing. North Korea went on something close to a war footing in early 1949 and throughout the summer of 1949 North and South Korean troops fought pitched battles along the 38th parallel. With many crack soldiers still in China, however, North Korea was not ready to fight in 1949.

The Rhee regime also wanted to unify Korea under its rule, by force if necessary. Rhee often referred to a "northern expedition" to "recover the lost territory," and in the summer of 1949 his army provoked the majority of the fighting along the 38th parallel (according to formerly secret American documents), fighting that took hundreds of lives from time to time. Rhee persistently asked various important Americans to provide the necessary military equipment to reunify the country. This was a prime reason why the United States refused to supply tanks and airplanes to the ROK: it feared that they would be used to invade the North. When Dean Acheson made a famous speech in January 1950 in which he appeared to place South Korea outside the American defense perimeter in Asia, he was seeking to remind Rhee that he could not count on automatic American backing, regardless of how he behaved. Other influential Americans made clear to Rhee that he would only be helped if there was an unprovoked invasion from the North.

Newly released documents from Moscow now show that Kim Il Sung succeeded where Rhee failed. He importuned Stalin many times for help in conquering the South, and after several refusals, Stalin finally agreed to have his advisers help the North plan an attack and to ship large quantities of military equipment to Pyongyang. He also told Kim to go to Beijing and consult with Mao in the spring of 1950, about which much less is known. Nor is it yet known why Stalin made these decisions; he might have thought that absorbing South Korea into the Communist sphere would be easy, or he might have hoped to pit China against the United States and thereby assure the new Chinese leadership's loyalty to the Soviet bloc. In any case, when Kim's regime was nearly extinguished in the fall of 1950 the Soviets did very little to save it. China picked up the pieces, and the North Koreans have never forgotten it. From that moment on, it was clear that North Korea treasured its relationship with China, whereas it dealt with the Soviet Union because it had to, not because it loved to.

Building Two States in One Country

Had there been no Soviet or American occupation, the effects of the colonial period would nonetheless have assured deep divisions within Korean society. The big powers did not invent communism and capitalism; Koreans had begun discovering both in the 1920s, if not earlier. The big powers could not press buttons and get their way; Koreans proved recalcitrant even to violent pressures.

The big powers chose to recognize 1948 as the year when separate regimes emerged—but that is only because the United States and the Soviet Union take credit for the establishment of the ROK and the DPRK. Actually, both regimes were in place, de facto, by the end of 1946. They each had bureaucracies, and police and military organizations, and thus effective political power. They each had preempted, or at least shaped, the Korea policies of the big powers.

In the South, the actual planning for a separate regime began in the last months of 1945. Syngman Rhee, a 70-year-old patriot who had lived in the United States since 1911 (when he earned a Ph.D. at Princeton University), returned in October with the backing of General MacArthur and elements in military and intelligence circles in the United States. A crusty and conservative man of the older generation, he was also a master politician. Within weeks he had won control of conservative and traditionalist factions, many of them from the landed class; he also had found friends among Americans worried about the spread of radicalism who needed little convincing that Rhee and his allies would be a bulwark against communism. In short order, the American occupation leaders and Rhee began to make plans for a separate administration of southern Korea, for a southern army (which began training in January 1946), for the reestablishment of a national police force, and for a "Koreanization" of the government bureaucracy left by the Japanese (which was substantially completed by the end of 1946). The Americans staffed the military, the police and the bureaucracy mostly with Koreans who had had experience in the colonial regime; they thought they had no other choice, but in so doing the regime took on a reactionary cast that weakened it in its competition with the North.

The Americans immediately ran into monumental opposition to such policies from the mass of South Koreans, leading to a sorry mess of strikes, violence, a massive rebellion in four provinces in the fall of 1946, and a significant guerrilla movement in 1948 and 1949. Much of this was due to the unresolved land problem, as conservative landowners used their bureaucratic power to block redistribution of land to tenants. The North Koreans, of course, sought to take advantage of this discontent, but the best evidence shows that most of the dissidents and guerrillas were southerners upset about southern policies. Indeed, the strength of the left wing was in those provinces most removed from the 38th parallel, in the southwest and the southeast.

We can see the general picture in some of the first CIA reports on Korea. In one 1948 document CIA analysts wrote that South Korean political life was "dominated by a rivalry between rightists and the remnants of the Left Wing People's Committees," which the CIA termed a "grass-roots independence movement which found expression in the establishment of the People's Committees throughout Korea in August 1945," led by "Communists" who based their right to rule on the resistance to the Japanese. The leadership of the right, on the other hand,

> ... is provided by that numerically small class which virtually monopolizes the native wealth and education of the country.... Since this class could not have acquired and maintained its favored position under Japanese rule without a certain minimum of 'collaboration,' it has ex-

Syngman Rhee, president of South Korea from 1948 to 1960, with General Douglas MacArthur.

perienced difficulty in finding acceptable candidates for political office and has been forced to support imported expatriate politicians such as Rhee Syngman and Kim Koo. These, while they have no pro-Japanese taint, are essentially demagogues bent on autocratic rule.

Thus, "the extreme rightists control the overt political structure in the United States zone," mainly through the agency of the National Police, which had been "ruthlessly brutal in suppressing disorder." The CIA went on to say,

The enforced alliance of the police with the right has been reflected in the cooperation of the police with rightist youth groups for the purpose of completely suppressing leftist activity. This alignment has had the effect of forcing the left to operate as an underground organization since it could not effectively compete in a parliamentary sense even if it should so desire.

By 1947, American authorities had come to understand that Rhee might hurt their cause more than help it. The commander of the occupation, General John R. Hodge, came to distrust and even detest Rhee.

33

Still, Rhee knew well that his great "hole card" was the wavering unreliability of more moderate politicians: they might prefer a unified Korea under Kim Il Sung to a separate South under Rhee. He parlayed this hole card into an American commitment to back the ROK in world forums, even to the point of getting the UN to bless his regime by observing an election and by de facto recognition.

The North Korean regime also emerged de facto in 1946. Within a year of liberation, the North had a powerful political party, a budding army, and the mixed blessing of a single leader named Kim Il Sung. Although Kim had rivals, one can date his emergence—and the Kim system that will be treated later on—from mid-1946. By then he had placed close, loyal allies at the heart of power. His prime assets were his anti-Japanese background, his organizational skills and his ideology. Although Kim was only 34 when he came to power, few other Koreans who were still alive could match his record of resistance to the Japanese. He was fortunate to emerge in the last decade of a 40-year resistance that had killed off many leaders of the older generation. The DPRK today absurdly claims that Kim was the leader of all Korean resisters, when in fact there were many. But he was able to win the support and firm loyalty of several hundred people like him: young, tough, nationalistic guerrillas who had fought in Manchuria. The prime test of legitimacy in postwar Korea was one's record under the hated Japanese regime. Kim and his core allies possessed nationalist credentials that were superior to those of the Rhee leadership. Furthermore, Kim's backers had military force at their disposal and used it to advantage against rivals with no military experience.

Kim's organizational skills probably came from his experience in the Chinese Communist party in the 1930s. Unlike traditional Korean leaders—and many more-intellectual or theoretical Communists—he pursued a style of mass leadership, using his considerable charisma, the practice of going down to the factory or the farm for "on-the-spot guidance," and encouraging his allies always to do the same. The North Koreans went against Soviet orthodoxy by including masses of poor peasants in the Korean Workers' party (KWP), indeed terming it a mass rather than a vanguard party. Since the 1940s the DPRK has enrolled 12 to 14 percent of the population in the dominant party, compared to 1 to 3 percent for most Communist parties. Data from captured documents show that the vast majority of party members have been poor peasants with no previous political experience. Membership in the party gave them position, prestige, privileges and a rudimentary form of political participation.

Kim's ideology tended to be revolutionary-nationalist rather than Communist. He talked about Korea, not about the Communist International. He spoke of unification, not national division. He discussed nationalism, not Marxism. He distributed land to the tillers instead of collectivizing it (at least until the Korean War began). One can also see in the late 1940s the beginnings of the Juche ideology so ubiquitous in North Korea today, a doctrine stressing self-reliance and independence.

Kim's greatest political weapon, however, was his control of the party and the army. He systematically filtered his allies through the commanding heights of each; when the Korean People's Army was founded in 1948 it was said to have grown out of Kim's guerrilla army and to have inherited its "revolutionary tradition." When masses of Koreans who fought with the Chinese Communists came back to Korea in 1949, and thereby threatened Kim's power, he had himself declared *suryong* or "supreme leader," a designation that had only been used for Stalin until that time.

Although there remain many murky aspects of the Korean War, it now seems that the frontal attack in June 1950 was mainly Kim's decision, to which he got Stalin's reluctant acquiescence, and that the key enabling factor was not Soviet weaponry (which the North already had in substantial amounts by the end of 1948), but the presence of as many as 100,000 troops with battle experience in China. When the Rhee regime, with help from American military advisers, largely eliminated the guerrilla threat in the winter of 1949–50, the civil war moved into a conventional phase. Had the Americans stayed out, the northern regime would have won easily; the southern army and state would have collapsed in a few days. As it happened, however, Kim's regime was nearly extinguished. When the war finally ended, the North had been devastated by three years of bombing attacks that left hardly a modern building standing. Both Koreas had watched as a virtual holocaust ravaged their country and turned the vibrant expectations of 1945 into a nightmare.

The point to remember is that it was a civil war and, as a British diplomat once said, "every country has a right to have its 'War of the Roses'." The true tragedy was not the war itself, for a civil conflict strictly among Koreans might have resolved the extraordinary tensions generated by colonialism and national division. The tragedy was that the war resolved nothing: only the status quo ante was restored. Today the tensions and the problems remain.

4

South Korean Politics

THE POST–KOREAN WAR ERA has been marked by relative political stability interrupted by periodic crises, making it difficult to characterize the period as a whole. South Korea has been more stable than many developing nations, which may suffer coups every six months. Yet every Korean republic until the one elected in 1993 under Kim Young Sam began or ended in massive street demonstrations or military coups. The best explanation for this pattern is probably the interplay of tensions generated by extraordinarily rapid change.

The ROK economy has gone from stagnant poverty to dynamic growth and considerable wealth in one generation; this is the most important single change (see Chapter 6). New political forces have emerged, the most important being the military and burgeoning middle and working classes. New institutions, from huge corporate conglomerates to the Korean Central Intelligence Agency (KCIA), have transformed the economy and the role of the state. The political system itself has changed dramatically. And new tensions have arisen in an older relationship, that between the United States and Korea.

The End of the Rhee Regime

American influence in the South was strong enough to shape the formal rules of the game of South Korean politics but not sufficient to affect the substance of politics. Thus the 1948 constitution read like a relatively liberal document, guaranteeing basic freedoms of speech and press, a vociferous legislature and periodic legislative elections. It had certain critical loopholes as well, allowing Rhee to proclaim emergencies or use draconian national-security laws to deal with his opposition. South Korea's intrepid journalists often criticized the regime in a press freer than South Korea subsequently permitted until the 1987 reforms, and freer than North Korea's in any period since 1945. Yet no one could call South Korea a liberal democracy before 1960, although many Americans hoped that it was at least moving in that direction. The extraordinary number of political executions and the thousands of political prisoners held in Rhee's jails led independent observers to label Rhee's Korea one of the worst authoritarian states in Asia.

The aged Rhee continued to rule in South Korea until 1960. He presided over war-torn devastation, reconstruction and rehabilitation, and relative economic stagnation. The Korean War did eliminate some recalcitrant problems, if violently. The paradoxical effect of the three-month North Korean occupation of the South in 1950 was to make possible a 1951 land reform and the end of landlord dominance in the countryside. Many landlords were eliminated and many more fled from the North Koreans; under much U.S. pressure, their land was redistributed to tenants. Thus the age-old balance between the central state and rural power was definitively transformed, and the state benefited. Also, the war effectively ended the strong threat from the left. Radical peasant and labor organizations, as well as the formerly strong guerrillas, had almost completely disappeared by the mid-1950s. The left's influence remained as an important residual or subliminal force, but it lacked organization and expression. This led to a diffuse authoritarianism in the period 1953–60, one that allowed a limited pluralism and a moderately free press; there was no space for leftists or independent labor unions, but perhaps a bit more than in the past for intellectuals, students and the moderate opposition.

What remained unchanged was the fundamental character of the

Rhee regime: its police and military holdovers from the colonial period, its authoritarian bent, its use of the state to preserve power rather than to stimulate the economy. Americans, in particular, were upset by the inability of Rhee and his allies to get the economy going and growing; furthermore, by the end of the war the United States had an immense military, political and administrative presence in Korea and provided about five sixths of the ROK's imports in direct grants and subsidies. It did not want this investment wasted, and therefore helped prepare the ground for a new, dynamic economic program.

In the spring of 1960 an electoral scandal triggered large student protests, joined at a critical point by university professors, that toppled the 85-year-old Rhee and his regime. Rhee retired to Hawaii, where he died in 1965, and the opposition came to power through what is known as the April Revolution. In many ways Korea's modern students have inherited the Confucian dictum that scholars should be activists in politics and moral examples to others. The year 1960 was one of their finest hours, and since that time they have often stood for—and suffered for—democratization and basic human rights. They and the common people who joined them during the April Revolution also made possible the partial completion of the 1945 agenda of liberation: the police and the army were finally purged of many Koreans who had served the Japanese.

The moderate opposition to the Rhee regime organized the Second Republic, which lasted less than a year until replaced by a military coup. The most democratic of Korea's postwar regimes, it was also the weakest. The Democratic party under Chang Myon had a majority, but it was basically the same conservative grouping of yangbans and landed gentry that had emerged in 1945. Americans tended to like this group far better than the Rhee group, and Chang was a particular favorite. His was seemingly the most liberal group. But the group's liberalism was weak, and it tended to oppose a strong executive. The inordinate influence of American thinking on its members caused other Koreans to question its nationalist credentials. During 1960–61 the Second Republic tolerated boisterous student demonstrations, interference with the parliament, a noisy press, and, as the year wore on, an increasingly radicalized segment that wanted unification talks with the North. Still, none of this justified the military's sudden intervention. Indeed, most observers thought the political system was stabilizing in the spring of 1961.

The Colonels in Politics, 1961–79

The night of the colonels came on May 16, 1961, in a virtually bloodless coup that ushered in something utterly new to Korean politics, a modern military organization of younger, nationalistic officers who were determined to quiet protest and build up the economy. Members of the second and eighth classes of the Korean Military Academy, who graduated in 1946 and 1949 respectively, put an end to the Chang regime. South Korea did not free itself of this military influence until 1993, when civilian politician Kim Young Sam was inaugurated. Retired generals still populate many major institutions in South Korea—the corporations, the National Assembly and much of political life as a whole.

The leader of this coup was Colonel Park Chung Hee, trained first by the Japanese and then the Americans, active in military intelligence during the Korean War, and, like many other officers of his generation, upset with the privileges, the corruption and the incompetence of senior military officials during the Rhee period. He ruled until 1963 according to a classic junta pattern, vowing to rid South Korea of corruption and get the economy moving.

Park donned civilian clothes and ran for election in 1963 under intense pressure from the Kennedy Administration to redress the human-rights violations. He won that election, and another in 1967, and still another in 1971. The 1963 election was perhaps the freest in postwar Korea, and it coincided with a new constitution, written with private American help, that sought to disperse and confine executive power in a stronger legislature and a two-party system that would legitimate a strong opposition. But as with the Chang regime, this reflected American preferences and was an index of South Korea's dependence upon the United States. Furthermore, this was a highly conditional democracy; most observers thought the military would step in again if Park somehow lost an election.

The eight-year period from 1963 to 1971 is relevant to South Korea today because the current system of military and business dominance within a competitive electoral system is quite similar. Although many pundits thought that 1987 marked Korea's first transition to democratic rule, the real transition did not come until 1993 and it returned the ROK to the politics of the 1960s: direct presidential elections, a functioning legislature, a moderately free press, all coexisting with authoritarian political structures like the still-extant National Security Law and the Agency for National Security Planning (ANSP), which remains strong today. The great achievement of Korean democracy in the 1990s has been to get the military out of politics, and that truly is something new.

Emergence of DRP and KCIA

President Park's political preferences were best represented in two new institutions that emerged in the 1960s, the ruling Democratic Republican party (DRP) and the KCIA. The former was really the first effective non-Communist political party in postwar Korea; it was modeled less on American parties than on the quasi-Leninist Kuomintang (or Nationalist party) of pre-Communist China, having a democratic-centralist internal structure, a permanent secretariat and an enormous funding base provided by the regime's private supporters and foreign friends in Japan and the United States. (Japanese sources pumped as much as $60 million into Park's political coffers in the early 1960s, and several American corporations added at least $10 million later on.) A critical problem of rapid development is to dovetail economic growth with an organization capable of channeling and containing newly mobilized forces in the interest of stability. The DRP was intended to be such an organization. It was also a personal political machine for Park, although its founder and an ally in the coup, Kim Jong-pil, soon came to rival Park for power.

Kim also was the organizer of the KCIA (with American CIA help), an agency that combined the functions of the American CIA and FBI, and broadened those activities as years went by. From the KCIA's inception, every one of its directors was a potential rival for presidential power, and in 1979 its director put an end to the Park regime by shooting Park to death over dinner one October night. Nonetheless, until the 1970s its role was relatively circumscribed; only after the political system itself changed did the KCIA become a dominant institution in Korean political life.

41

A new, formally authoritarian political system emerged in 1971–72, known as the Yushin (revitalizing) system. By the end of 1972, the National Assembly had become a creature of executive power—a rubber stamp; indirect presidential elections replaced the direct vote and made Park in effect president-for-life; the regime muzzled the press and intellectual dissent by stationing KCIA officers and censors in newspaper offices and universities; the opposition parties were systematically surveilled and harassed, leading to the kidnapping of Kim Dae Jung in Tokyo in August 1973; finally dissidents were subjected to torture that made South Korea a target of Amnesty International (an organization that seeks the release of political prisoners), and a prime problem for American policy.

South Korean citizens believed that the best way to deal with KCIA surveillance was "not to talk about anything at all to anybody," even the members of one's family. The KCIA also began operating fairly openly in the United States and other countries, intimidating Korean communities abroad and even attempting to bribe congressmen. The latter effort extended beyond Congress to business and academic circles; when this large influence-buying effort became public in the course of congressional and Justice Department investigations, it got the title Koreagate and deeply affected Korean-American relations in the mid-1970s. As late as 1989, intelligence operatives in Korean consulates in the United States still openly intimidated Korean-American communities.

What were the reasons for this qualitative change in Korean politics, away from at least formal democratic procedure, toward substantive and frank authoritarianism? The obvious explanation is the threat to Park's rule posed by the 1971 election. Kim Dae Jung, a young charismatic leader from the southwestern provinces, had breathed life into the opposition, and, unlike previous opposition candidates, he could not be linked to the hated colonial period or to the struggles in the 1940s to preserve the power of the landowners. He got 46 percent of the vote, in spite of widespread attempts by the regime to manipulate the election, buy votes and mobilize supporters at the polls. There were deeper reasons as well.

Park himself cited the changing international environment as his justification for Yushin, and indeed 1971–72 did bring big changes. The

Nixon Administration opened relations with China (North Korea's ally); began to withdraw a division of American troops from South Korea; and bargained hard on South Korean textile exports to the U.S. market. For the first time since 1953, the ROK could not count on automatic American backing: the cold war was ending around Korea, if not in Korea. This was a key reason for Koreagate: the Park regime sought to reverse Richard M. Nixon's decisions in Congress and shore up its support in other American circles.

The Third Five-Year Plan, 1971–76, had inaugurated a phase of heavy industrialization: new steel, petrochemical, auto, shipbuilding and nuclear industries were part of this audacious program, devised by economic nationalists who resented Korea's dependence on outside sources for heavy industrial materials. American planners resisted these developments, arguing that Korea's small domestic market and limited endowments would lead to problems of surplus and idle capacity. Park, however, clearly sided with the economic nationalists. In a pithy 1972 slogan he declared that "steel equals national power" and laced his rhetoric with calls for self-reliance and for "Korean-style" politics.

Although all of these factors played a part in the emergence of authoritarianism, the most important were the deepening industrialization program and the repression of groups opposed to this course, such as labor unions and small businesses. A daunting paradox of Yushin was that the ROK became more authoritarian as its economy became more successful, exactly the reverse of what American liberals had hoped for. South Korea had been more democratic when it had a per capita income of $200 in 1960 than it was with a per capita income of $800 in 1978.

The 1980s: The Colonels Again

In the spring of 1979, with economic problems mounting and no relaxation of political restrictions, a crisis erupted that destroyed the Park regime. In the late spring of 1987, with the economy booming and in a period of political relaxation, another crisis felled Park's successor, Chun Doo Hwan. Only in 1992 did the Korean people finally elect a civilian president amid general political stability.

The 1979 problems began with markedly enhanced opposition

power deployed around Kim Dae Jung, who drew support from textile workers, students and intellectuals, small businesses and firms with national rather than international interests, and from his native southwestern region that had historically been rebellious and had not benefited from most of the growth of the previous 15 years. (Park, like his successors Chun and Roh, was from the southeast and had poured all sorts of investment into that region.) In circumstances that remain mysterious but appear to be related to dissatisfaction with the way Park was handling all the dissent, KCIA director Kim Jae Kyu shot Park to death on the night of October 26 and then was himself arrested in what seemed to have been a bungled coup attempt. Nonetheless, the regime collapsed and thereby demonstrated how much ROK politics still depended on firm control by a single leader. The investigation into the assassination was headed by Major General Chun Doo Hwan, who was then chief of the powerful Defense Security Command and a longtime protégé of Park Chung Hee.

The next night of the colonels (young officers who were actually generals by then) occurred on December 12, 1979, when Gen. Chun and his close friend Gen. Roh executed a coup within the Korean military that slowly brought to power the 1955 graduating class of the Korean Military Academy (of which both were members). They mobilized armored units in front of the ROK Army headquarters, forcing its high officers to flee through tunnels to the American Eighth Army Command across the street. A 1994 National Assembly report called this a "premeditated military rebellion" and a "coup-like event," but the 38 officers who led it were never punished.

During the early months of 1980, South Koreans met openly to discuss a new constitution, and although students were quite active on Seoul's campuses, they sought not to provoke the situation by moving out into the streets. In late April, however, miners seized a small town and held it for a week, and Chun had himself declared head of the KCIA. Thereupon, students and commoners poured into the streets. In mid-May hundreds of thousands of protesters in Seoul mounted demonstrations unprecedented since 1960. Martial law was declared, which in turn touched off a rebellion in the southwest, centered in the provincial capital of Kwangju. Rebels held the city and some surrounding towns for a week. Chun and his allies put down the rebellion with

Arrested students are led away by ROK soldiers in Kwangju in May 1980 after the country's bloodiest antigovernment rebellion since the Korean War.

great brutality and loss of life: official figures say 200 civilians died, but dissidents say as many as 2,000; in the 1990s it was learned that Kwangju's mortality statistics, which ordinarily averaged 2,300 monthly, soared to 4,900 in May 1980.

The Kwangju rebellion was the worst political calamity in the ROK since the Korean War. For young people, in particular, Kwangju became a touchstone as important to their political consciousness as the Korean War was to their parents' and opened a deep generational gulf in Korean politics. In many ways, Kwangju was the "Tiananmen Square" of Korean politics, bearing close comparison to the Chinese crackdown on students and workers in Beijing in June 1989.

Chun had himself inaugurated president in February 1981. In the same year he purged or proscribed the political activities of 800 politicians, 8,000 government and business officials, and threw some 37,000 journalists, students, teachers, labor organizers and civil servants into "purification camps" in remote mountain areas. Chun then proclaimed a "new era" and, on the surface, politics returned to a pattern of stabil-

45

ity marked by minor demonstrations and strikes. A new political elite emerged, along with wholly new political parties. Chun abolished some of the more absurd manifestations of authoritarianism, such as the nightly curfew that had been in effect since 1945 and the Japanese-military-style uniforms that all schoolboys used to wear. But the political system remained fundamentally Park's Yushin system in a new guise. In spite of much commentary about South Korea's political "maturity" under Chun (all too much of it coming from official and unofficial American friends), he ended up as the most unpopular leader in postwar Korean history, reviled as much for his lack of imagination and his slavish attempts to mimic Park Chung Hee's politics as for his draconian measures. All this provoked another crisis in the mid-1980s.

With much fanfare Chun had declared that at the end of his term he would voluntarily step down and thus arrange South Korea's first stable leadership transition. Repressive measures against the opposition were also diminished, allowing Kim Dae Jung to return from his American exile in early 1985 (if only to prolonged house arrest). This modest relaxation seemed to stimulate popular political appetites; in National Assembly elections held in February 1985, participation was high and the opposition did far better than anyone expected, given the system's structured favoritism toward those in power. This was really the beginning of the end of the Chun regime. It turned out that Chun's concept was to have the ruling party endorse Roh Tae Woo as his chosen successor, which it did in June 1987.

This provoked massive urban demonstrations throughout South Korea, stimulated first by student hunger strikers but later joined by many middle-class adults. The Korean insurrection was quite similar to the large demonstrations that brought down several East European Communist dictatorships in 1989.

Movement toward Democratic Politics

In late June, with big cities paralyzed by demonstrators and with newspapers full of rumors of a military coup, Roh suddenly announced direct elections for the presidency and proceeded to lift most of the restrictions on political activity. The regime also removed controls on organizing labor in the summer of 1987. From June 1987 to June 1988, unions increased membership by 64 percent, adding 586,167 new recruits; some 3,400 labor disputes, strikes and lockouts occurred from July through October 1987, involving 934,000 workers. Most labor disputes were about wages, but this was a historic advance for South Korean labor.

Roh proved himself a far better politician than the taciturn and unloved Chun; his dramatic and shrewd stroke plunked the ball firmly in the opposition's court, and the opposition proceeded to bobble it. Through endless name changes and equally endless bickering, the opposition parties proved to be little different from what they were in the 1950s and 1960s: groups held together by a strong leader, not effective political organizations. As the December 1987 elections approached, Kim Dae Jung and the other major opposition figure, Kim Young Sam, were unable to agree on a single candidate to challenge the incumbents. So they renamed their parties and ran separately, yielding the predictable result of splitting the opposition vote and allowing the Chun-Roh forces to remain in power. (Roh got 37 percent of the vote, and the two Kims neatly divided most of the remainder.) They compounded the blunder in the April 1988 National Assembly elections, splitting 129 seats between them while the ruling party got only 125 of the 299 seats. In 1990 Kim Young Sam finally threw his fortunes in with the ruling group, joining Roh (and a resurgent Park-era figure, Kim Jong-pil) in yet another new party, the Democratic Liberal party (DLP). This proved to be a shrewd move, for it finally enabled Kim Young Sam to win a presidency he had sought since his youngest days, when he was a protégé of Chang Taek-sang (who ran the Seoul Metropolitan Police under the U.S. occupation).

The events of 1987 did not signal South Korea's first successful leadership "transition," but they did embody a real movement in the direction of democratic politics. Although direct presidential elections had to be forced on a very reluctant leadership by massive street protests, since that time South Korea has made steady political progress. Above all, after his inauguration in 1993, President Kim Young Sam moved deftly to get South Korea's strong military back to the barracks and back to its proper role of defending the ROK. Electoral politics is now very lively in South Korea, the press is much freer, and sharp disputes between the executive and the legislature indicate a developing dispersion of power from the center.

Still, the political system has proved incapable as yet of shaking the dominance of the southeastern elites and former high-ranking military officers who have been in power since 1961. They continue to hold many Cabinet posts. If the old days of authoritarian dictate are over, most of the institutions built during the Park years still exist. The National Security Law is still used to suppress unorthodox views: all through the summer of 1994, for example, people who tried to send condolences to Pyongyang after the death of Kim were marched off to jail under this law, and in August the U.S. State Department publicly called for its abrogation.

Four Constants

There are some constants to be pointed out in South Korean politics from 1961 to 1995. First, although it is back in the barracks, the military still remains a powerful force, as do the intelligence and national security bureaucracies. Second, the wealth of South Korea's big corporations has stood behind the ruling party for three decades, but it has also been manifest in politics in recent years (particularly when Hyundai chairman Chung Ju Yung ran unsuccessfully for president in 1992). Third, powerful groups continue to show regional divisions: the southeastern Kyongsang provinces have been vastly overrepresented both in the leadership and in state and corporate investments. (This was an important reason for the southwestern rebellion in 1980.) Fourth, a profound hostility continues to exist between military and intelligence officers (who are primarily of nonyangban, peasant stock) and students, intellectuals and much of the opposition (with backgrounds that more often tend to be yangban who share the Confucian sense that scholars should be moral leaders and should disdain the military arts).

The political system still does not have viable political parties. Although the ruling party is always the strongest by virtue of its state support and superior funding, it has not yet constituted itself as a core element of stable politics. Opposition parties tend to continue the old pattern of patron-client ties in which factions cluster around a single leader. Voting has been of central importance to the system since 1985, and various groups now articulate strong preferences, but the ruling party continues to rely on what some scholars have called mobilized

Kim Young Sam (l.), President Roh Tae Woo (c.) and Kim
Jong-pil (r.) at an inauguration party for new coalition
government in February 1990.

voting, that is, people go to the polls because they are ordered to, or
because they are paid to go, not because they have much sense of
participation.

At this writing, South Korean politics revolves around "three Kims"
who have been prominent since the 1960s: president Kim, opposition
leader Kim Dae Jung, and ruling DLP chairman Kim Jong-pil—Park
Chung Hee's old comrade-in-arms. Nonetheless the Kim Young Sam
administration holds the promise of moving forward to a truly new era
of competitive politics. One way this would happen is for the ruling
DLP to succeed in providing stable, one-party democratic rule on the
Japanese pattern. The DLP is clearly modeled on the Liberal Democratic party (LDP), which held sway in Japan from 1955 to 1993; no
doubt Korea's growing middle class would like a long period of stability, since it now finds its interests represented in the National Assembly. Labor is still excluded from the ruling coalition, however, and still
cannot legally engage in open partisan politics (labor unions are pro-

hibited by law from giving their funds to any parties or candidates, and from fielding candidates themselves). Yet labor grows in numbers and power every year. Japan under LDP rule neither excluded labor from "peak" political arrangements nor did it have laws on its books (like the National Security Law) that cancelled basic political rights. The stark regional voting patterns of the past decade also do not augur well for long-term DLP rule. The legislature, while including many former dissidents and opposition figures, remains basically "a conservative club," in the words of political scientist Park Kie-duck, as it has been since its inception in 1948.

A new era would also arrive, however, if the long-excluded opposition forces win power. The ruling party faces the likely prospect that its candidate will run against an opposition group finally united behind Kim Dae Jung in the next presidential elections, scheduled for 1997. If Kim Dae Jung or another strong opposition candidate sinks his roots in South Korea's vast laboring class, another important transition toward full democracy may come in 1997.

South Korea's new civilian politics is unquestionably a great success, regardless of who wins the next election. But it took a very long time in coming and required the stalwart willingness of millions of ordinary Koreans to struggle for democracy and basic human rights over a period of nearly 50 years.

5

North Korean Politics

THE DEMOCRATIC People's Republic of Korea has a political system that is not easy to understand, to state the case mildly. It is among the world's most closed, impenetrable regimes, with a totally controlled press, sharp restrictions on travel into, out of, and around the country, few "listening points" (like Hong Kong for China) where defectors collect, and an ideology of self-reliance that often matches the "exclusionism" of the Yi period. North Korea is often thought to be about the worst place in the world: it is only matched by Pol Pot's Cambodia, former Secretary of State Henry Kissinger told the author in an interview. The DPRK is not the worst place in the world, but it is hard for outsiders to know that, and the regime does not make knowing it easy.

North Korea is startlingly different, like Pyongyang's 105-story pyramid-shaped "international hotel." According to regime scribes, it is the tallest building in Asia, but it is empty inside.

In 1981, several guides chaperoned the author everywhere. During a much longer visit in 1987, when he accompanied a documentary film crew, he was able to walk around freely and talk to ordinary citizens. Still, he had the feeling of observing a movie set, with a series of performances put on for the foreigner's benefit. How can one know anything about this isolated country?

There is one fascinating window on the DPRK, provided by a large collection of documents captured during the Korean War. These documents, combined with the chaperoned visits and frequent and careful reading of the official press, make possible some generalizations. The first generalization is that because of the extraordinary longevity and relative stability of the regime, its origins in the 1940s can tell us much today. The supreme leader, Kim Il Sung, came into effective power in early 1946 and only relinquished it when he died in 1994. He always surrounded himself with comrades connected to the guerrilla struggle against Japan; although many are now dead, including O Jin-u who for many years commanded North Korea's million-strong military and who passed away in February 1995, others remain and all of them established their families and friends at the commanding heights of the regime. In the 1940s and 1950s Kim Il Sung faced power struggles between his guerrilla group and other Communists, but these ensued during only the first decade of the regime and were essentially finished by the mid-1950s; meanwhile Kim and his allies solidified controls at the center and made everyone's career dependent on their blessings thereafter. It is known of course that there were conflicts within the leadership, but they have been relatively minor and have not successfully challenged what can be nicknamed Kimist political power. Thus what is known of the origins of the regime can say much about the contemporary regime as well.

The DPRK originated in a period of maximum Soviet influence and therefore had the typical structure associated with all Marxist-Leninist regimes: a strong, highly organized party; centralized, top-down administration by weighty bureaucracies; an economy in which goods and services were allocated according to central, long-term plans rather than market principles; collectivized agriculture and priority of heavy industry over light; and an ideology traced to Marx and Lenin that placed the DPRK in the stage of "building socialism" toward a distant final transition to communism.

It all seems quaint now; the highest stage of "socialism" turned out to be capitalism for the U.S.S.R. and its European allies. Most of the Communist regimes with a similar birth and structure are now historical artifacts, museum pieces. So why is the DPRK still in power? Why has it not collapsed, as many analysts in 1989 predicted it would? One answer is that "the East is still Red." There has been no break in East Asian communism save for the predictable case of Mongolia, which was always tied closely to Moscow. As long as Communists continue to hold power in China, North Korea still has a powerful ally. Although many observers thought Beijing would wash its hands of North Korea after it normalized relations with Seoul, it has followed a policy closer to equidistance between the two Koreas, no doubt because North Korea is one of the world's last redoubts of communism. This makes Pyongyang's predicament much less dire than Cuba's, for example.

More important to its survival, however, is that North Korea was never a typical Communist state. Marxism presented no political model for achieving socialism, only an opaque set of prescriptions. This political vacuum opened the way to an assertion of indigenous political culture, and may even demand it by virtue of the very paucity of political models. If the DPRK leadership was influenced by any foreign model, it was the Chinese Communist one. Kim Il Sung was very much a "mass line" leader like Mao, making frequent visits to factories and the countryside, sending cadres down to local levels to help implement policy and to solicit local opinion, requiring small-group political study and so-called criticism and self-criticism, using periodic campaigns to mobilize people for production or education, and encouraging soldiers to engage in production in good "people's army" fashion.

But that explanation is also unsatisfying, especially since China gave up most of its Maoist policies after Mao's death in 1976. The truth is that North Korea has drawn deeply from the well of nationalism and from historical Korean political practice to fill the Marxist vacuum, and this is the main reason why its system has not yet collapsed.

Confucian Communism

The symbol of the Korean Workers' party (KWP), a hammer and sickle with a writing brush superimposed, is supposed to represent the "three-class alliance" of workers, peasants and intellectuals. Unlike

Mao's China, the Kim regime never excoriated intellectuals as a potential "new class" of exploiters; instead, from the beginning it followed an inclusive policy toward them, perhaps because postwar Korea was so short of intellectuals and experts, and because so many left the North for the South in the 1945–50 period; but it is also because Koreans have so much respect for the wielders of the writing brush, namely, the old scholar-officials. (The term intellectual, of course, refers to experts and technocrats, not dissenters and critics, of which there are exceedingly few in North Korea, even when compared to China and the former Soviet Union. But then there were not many in the Yi Dynasty, either.)

In contrast to the typical Marxist-Leninist model, the KWP is less a tiny vanguard than a big "mass party," as mentioned earlier, which then raises the question, what is the vanguard? It is what Kim calls the core or nucleus at the commanding heights of the regime, consisting of himself and his closest associates. All "good things" emanate in top-down fashion from this core, in sharp departure from Maoist dicta about the source of good ideas being the mass of peasants and workers. But this principle of core leadership is just the beginning of the DPRK's unique political system, and it is here that indigenous Korean political culture is most pronounced.

North Korean ideology has supplanted Marxism-Leninism with a ubiquitous, always-trumpeted Juche ideology, a doctrine calling for autonomy at home and self-reliance and independence vis-à-vis the rest of the world. One cannot open a DPRK newspaper or listen to a single speech without hearing about Juche. The North Koreans fund and organize Juche study groups all over the world. The term was first used in a 1955 speech in which Kim castigated some of his comrades for being too pro-Soviet—thinking that if the Soviets eat fish on Monday, Koreans should too. But it really means placing all foreigners at arm's length and resonates deeply with Korea's Hermit Kingdom past.

North Korea's nationalism and tight unity at home have produced a remarkably organic politics unprecedented in any other Communist regime. Kim Il Sung was not just the "iron-willed, ever-victorious commander," the "respected and beloved Leader"; he was also the "head and heart" of the body politic, even "the supreme brain of the nation"—a mantle now held by his son, Kim Jong Il. The flavor of this politics can only be gotten through quotation from party newspapers at the time Kim's son was anointed as his chosen successor:

> *Kim Il Sung ... is the great father of our people....Long is the history of the word father being used as a word representing love and reverence ... expressing the unbreakable blood ties between the people and the leader. Father. This familiar word represents our people's single heart of boundless respect and loyalty.... The love shown by the Great Leader for our people is the love of kinship. Our respected and beloved Leader is the tender-hearted father of all the people.... Love of paternity ... is the noblest ideological sentiment possessed only by our people....*
>
> *His heart is a traction power attracting the hearts of all people and a centripetal force uniting them as one.... Kim Il Sung is the great sun and great man ... thanks to this great heart, national independence is firmly guaranteed.*

The party is referred to as the "Mother" party, the party line is said to provide "blood ties," the leader is always "fatherly," and the country is a kind of family-state, like the prewar Japanese ideal. The leader is said to be paternal and devoted and benevolent, and the people supposedly respond with loyalty, obedience and mutual love. This rhetoric has escalated as the transition to Kim Jong Il goes forward. Since 1989 many articles have called for all citizens to show "filial devotion" to Kim and/or his son, "the tender-hearted father who gave a genuine life" to them. In this way the regime draws upon the deepest wellsprings of morality animating the Korean people, namely, filial piety toward one's parents.

The succession to power of Kim Jong Il would not surprise any Korean king of the past two millennia, even if its success in 1994–95 surprised many foreign observers. The whole point of the old monarchy was to groom the king's first son to succeed him, just as founders of South Korea's conglomerates prepare their sons for succession, and just as the first son in Korean families inherits his father's authority and often lives with his wife under the parental roof. Kim Jong Il was publicly named at the Sixth Congress of the KWP in 1980 to the Presidium of the Politburo, the Secretariat of the Central Committee and the Military Commission. That is, he was openly designated successor to his father 15 years before his father died, but specialists had been able to spot this pattern of succession at least as early as 1970. The ground was carefully prepared throughout the past quarter century: by 1972 specialists could already see Jong Il's presence in important campaigns at the grass-roots level and in party organizational work, and his rise to power was carefully coordinated with party control.

Kim Jong Il, first son to Kim Il Sung, according to Pyongyang, was born in 1941 on the slopes of that great symbol of the Korean nation, Paektusan, or White Head Mountain, along the Sino-Korean border; Seoul, however, says he was born in the depths of Siberia. Neither is telling the truth: he was born at the camp near Khabarovsk where his father spent the latter years of World War II. His mother, Kim Jong-suk, was a guerrilla fighter who died in the late 1940s and unquestionably was no imposter, since her son looks just like her. By the time his father died, Jong Il ranked second in the leadership, behind his father and ahead of his father's old comrade-in-arms, O Jin-u. When O Jin-u passed on, Kim Jong Il was left alone among the three leaders who had dominated North Korea since the early 1980s. At this writing there is no evidence of serious opposition to him, and probably after a prolonged period of mourning (appropriate to a first son), he will get the remaining titles that have eluded him: chairman of the party and president of the state. It seems that from the time of his coming of age in the 1960s—or perhaps from time immemorial—every North Korean has known that Kim Jong Il was going to succeed his father.

Kim Il Sung's family is, of course, the model family—including his parents, grandparents, great-grandparents and numerous other relatives, all of whom were appropriately "revolutionary" and dedicated to Korea's independence. His great-grandfather is said to have led the charge against an American warship that steamed up the Taedong River in 1866. Unlike the Maoists, the regime has never tampered with the family affairs of its citizenry, and indeed the family is termed the core unit of society in the constitution, and the society as a whole is known as a great integrated entity—a family-state, at least in the minds of North Korean ideologues.

The DPRK ideologues also routinely tout a pronounced voluntarism—the theory that will is the dominant factor in the world. It is also characteristic of corporate politics. The Korean propagandists

DPRK President
Kim Il Sung in a
1994 photo with
his son and
successor,
Kim Jong Il.

say that "everything is decided by idea," directly contradicting the materialism at the heart of Marxism. And, of course, the leader's ideas are the best, compounded by his firm will, always described as ironlike, or steely. Kim invented Juche, and all Koreans "must have Juche firm in mind and spirit," and only then can they be good "Kimilsungists," and only then can the revolution be successful. Under the old monarchies, the kings and their scholar-offical scribes were also founts of clairvoyant ideas, and all the people were to imbibe them thus to create "one mind with the king."

The more one seeks to understand Juche, the more the meaning recedes. It is a state of mind, not an idea, and one that is unavailable to the non-Korean. It is the opaque core of what one could call North Korean national solipsism. Anyone familiar with North Koreans is struck by their combination of recalcitrance—a willingness to go their own way come hell or high water—and their corresponding conviction, one that often strikes foreigners as absurd, that North Korea is a model country for the whole world, which the whole world is watching. It once was a model for the Third World, to be sure, back in the 1960s and 1970s; "Che" Guevara visited Pyongyang in the 1960s and

57

proclaimed it a vision of what Cuba would eventually become, and socialist economist Joan Robinson called it a "miracle" economy. In the 1990s this rhetoric not only seems anachronistic, but it smacks of the way in which the Yi Dynasty held out to the very last against the encroaching West, mistaking the West's relative inattention for Korea's successful perseverance.

In 1990 when so many Marxist-Leninist systems had collapsed, the North Koreans proudly stated that they were still hewing to their well-worn path of "nation-first-ism," placing the nation first in everything. (So is this socialism, or nationalism? The answer is both.) The DPRK difference can only be explained by reference to the tradition and the political culture from whence it came. It is a mixture of Confucian holdovers, Korean traditionalism and socialist corporatism. The strength and stability of the system rest on marrying traditional forms of legitimacy to modern bureaucratic structures, with the peculiar charisma of Kim Il Sung having provided the transition and the glue between the two. The weakness is that core political power still rests upon family and personalistic ties, with trust barely extending beyond the leader's family and his longtime associates.

A 'Rogue State'?

This look inside North Korea may or may not explain why the DPRK is so reviled in the West. In any case, its external policy frequently gives good reasons for reviling it and explains why since 1989 it has been a charter member of an American-defined collection of renegade or "rogue" states. In October 1983 a bomb blast in Rangoon, Burma, decimated Chun Doo Hwan's Cabinet and very nearly killed Chun himself. A Burmese court determined that North Korean terrorists carried out this despicable act. The North Koreans presumably acted on the assumption that killing Chun would have an effect similar to the Park assassination in 1979: the removal of the supreme leader would disrupt the political system. They were probably right, sad to say. In 1987 another terrorist blew a South Korean airliner apart, an act also linked to North Korea. The motive for that act was much more murky; perhaps it was intended to dissuade foreigners from attending the 1988 Olympics in Seoul. If so, it bespoke desperation and a purely malicious and gratuitous terrorism. Although similar acts have not oc-

curred since 1987, North Korea until 1994 continued to export missiles and anything else it could sell for hard cash to like-minded regimes in the Middle East.

The DPRK has long been a significant actor in international arms-trafficking, selling machine guns, artillery, light tanks and other items to friendly countries such as Zimbabwe and Iran. (North Korea traded weaponry for oil with Iran, accounting for as much as 40 percent of Iranian arms imports during the long Iran-Iraq war.) According to U.S. intelligence, it has transshipped Chinese Silkworm missiles to the Middle East and sells improved SCUD missiles of its own design. In June 1993 the North launched a medium-range test missile called the Nodong 1 (Nodong means "worker") that went more than 300 miles downrange and hit the target right on the nose, sending a chill up Japanese spines since the full range of the missile (600+ miles) would open several Japanese cities to North Korean targeting. Foreign experts are not sure whether the precise targeting of the missile was an accident, or an indication of quite inexplicable technological prowess.

With its external reputation for terrorism and worst-case socialism, most observers after 1989 thought North Korea would go the way of the Stalinist states of Eastern Europe: collapse. Some thought Germany would be the model, with North Korea folding up like East Germany and being absorbed by the South. Others suggested the example of Romania, where President Nicolae Ceausescu had modeled his dictatorial rule on Kim Il Sung's example. The "revolution of 89" was so unexpected that it bred humility in all observers of socialist states. But it seems unlikely that North Korea will follow the East German path. It was Soviet President Mikhail S. Gorbachev who pulled the plug there. Amid the widespread demonstrations against Erich Honecker's regime, he kept the Soviet Army in the barracks. Furthermore, South Korea flatters itself with comparisons to West Germany; it has no social safety net like West Germany, something that attracted many Easterners who still believed in socialism. North Korea, moreover, has an independently controlled army rumored to be a million strong. It is very hard to believe that army commanders who fought the South in a bloody civil war would allow the ROK to overwhelm the DPRK, by whatever means, or simply yell "Uncle" and fold themselves into the southern army.

The Romanian example is more compelling. Ceausescu's collapse seemed to shock Pyongyang in December 1989, and there are unquestionably large numbers of North Koreans who would like to get the Kimist regime off their backs. Ceausescu, however, made the mistake of driving down living standards for a decade, something few regimes of any type could survive; North Korean living standards have always been low but have gone up incrementally. The economic crisis of the 1990s, about which more below, raises again the specter of a Romanian-style collapse. The author's prediction is that if the regime goes down, it will go down fighting. Better, therefore, to find less violent ways to bring North Korea out of its contemporary isolation.

Fallen Sun-King

Kim Il Sung, "Sun of the Nation," died of a heart attack on July 8, 1994. With Cable News Network cameras in Pyongyang, the world was able to watch an outpouring of grief that seemed, for such a reviled dictator, incomprehensible. Many thought the regime staged it, but how? Thousands of people were weeping and tearing their hair out all over the city. Mourning lasted for 100 days, and when it ended, a government spokesman said this:

> The loss of the great leader was the irretrievable loss of our people. At this shocking news, like the earth breaking apart and the sun falling, not only our party members and working people as well as the South Korean people and overseas compatriots, but even the mountains, rivers, plants, and trees wailed.

It was a shock, no doubt about it. Kim had placed his personal stamp on the DPRK like no other leader in our time. But the mourning hysterics were part and parcel of an old and venerable Korean tradition. Here again is Hendrik Hamel in 1656: "As soon as one dies, his Kindred run about the Streets shrieking, and tearing their Hair."

In the fall of 1994 an article in the party newspaper hailed Kim Jong Il's leadership qualities:

> The Dear Leader Comrade Kim Jong Il's iron will has become a boundless source of might to turn misfortune into a blessing.... The Great Leader Comrade Kim Il Sung has taught: Comrade Kim Jong Il has an invincible will, courage, outstanding strategy, and commanding art as befitting the supreme commander of the revolutionary Armed Forces.... The leader's will plays a decisive role in pioneering the destiny of one nation and in carrying out the socialist cause.... The leader is the supreme mind of the popular mass....

To the extent that statements like this constitute evidence, there is nothing today to suggest that the DPRK will soon depart from its long-standing policies of Confucian-linked corporate politics and leader-worship. But it faces immense problems. Designed to remedy the problems of the 1930s when the world economy had collapsed, the DPRK political economy now faces a very different 1990s. Its economy must produce and export much more in order to import the technology it must have to modernize its industrial base. Its long-standing foreign policy of self-reliance, combined with tilting between Moscow and Beijing, is clearly in a shambles in the 1990s; Beijing is

Pyongyang's only ally, and an unreliable one at that. Meanwhile Moscow and Beijing both try to cultivate ever deeper economic ties with Seoul. The world today seems more inhospitable to Pyongyang's policies than at any point since 1948. Will the regime survive to greet the millennium?

In the past, foreign observers have gone wrong in underestimating this regime in nearly every way possible. Meanwhile, predictions based on the idea that this regime draws deeply from the well of Korean nationalism and political tradition and will therefore have staying power in the post-cold-war world have been correct for six years. This cloistered regime faced the death of its founding father and remained stable, while passing on the baton to Kim Jong Il. How long it will last can be anybody's guess, but if Korean history is any guide, Kim Jong Il may well hand his baton to another son-king in the next century. Korea is not Eastern Europe. It suffered a terrible civil war, with millions killed, in recent history and recent memory.

It is therefore likely that instead of a North Korean collapse, the Korean peninsula will see more of the same in the near term of the next decade: continued division between North and South, with some warming of relations and increased inter-Korean exchange; more North Korean economic contact with the outside world and more involvement with the dynamic economies of East Asia; and the continued danger that if the regime thinks it is going down, it will go down fighting.

6

The Two Economies

THE TWO KOREAN ECONOMIES present great contrasts.One has an export-led system, the other a heavy-industry-led system. One is enmeshed in the world economy, the other seeks self-reliance. One has an open door, the other a closed door. Consumer goods and conspicuous wealth prevail in the South, capital goods and a chaste egalitarianism in the North. Seoul is a modern cosmopolitan city, a bustling megalopolis; Pyongyang has an austere, antiquarian atmosphere and a sparse, if busy, population. The ROK has witnessed a "miracle on the Han" in economic development, whereas the DPRK is lagging far behind, deeply in debt, and seemingly unable to escape relative stagnation.

On closer inspection, however, some of the differences give way to similarities. Seoul has pushed heavy industry for the past 25 years. Pyongyang has made exports a priority since the mid-1980s. The North imported an entire pantyhose factory in the early 1970s, just as the South began talking about self-reliance. Both governments play a determining role in the economy. The model villages and homes that both regimes show foreigners as indexes of modernization turn out to be nearly identical—even in architecture and taste. In both capital cities one can see elite Koreans pulling up to a barber shop in a shiny new Mercedes and jump inside for the latest razor cut. Both have officials who look and act like typical middle-class professionals the world over (although of course the South has many more). Both want to show the visitor their latest advanced technology (and in both cases it is often based on imported innards). Finally, neither side has produced a miracle, but both have been among the leading cases of rapid economic development. The North's problem is that its heyday of rapid growth ended by 1980, whereas the South has been a lodestar of rapid industrialization since 1965.

The Export-Driven South

How does one explain the unexpected outcome of a Republic of Korea that now has a gross domestic product (GDP) approaching the size of Spain's? It lacked domestic capital, crucial natural resources and a strong entrepreneurial class. U.S. Agency for International Development (AID) officials thought it was a basket case with little future, at least until the mid-1960s.

The ROK did have a strong state, which found a way to use foreign capital and earnings both to reward its friends and promote efficient production. It fostered one rising industry after another, starting with simple assembly operations and ending with gigaflop microprocessors etched in infinitesimally small lines on silicon wafers. It created from scratch octopus-like firms now known to the world as *chaebol* (the Korean word for zaibatsu). In conditions of often stunning political and social dislocation, it worked effectively to build support and slowly to legitimate its hell-bent-for-leather development program. Ultimately it will wrest from the great powers who divided it a unified Korea which will be among the advanced industrial nations of the next century.

Political scientist Woo Jung-en suggests several causes of this growth that seem at first glance highly unlikely: that Japanese imperialism did not just take but gave—as in "a colonially bequeathed strong state"; that Korea grew precisely *because* it lacked a class of capitalists, local versions of which kept getting in the way of growth in, say, Latin America; that cultural factors like Confucianism, Protestant ethics and work ethics neither hindered nor helped this process; that "foreign capital," which one radical after another has railed about since the first banker made a loan to a foreign country, was systematically put to good and different use by precisely the central government bureaucrats whom free-market economists always revile; not to mention that the ROK grew by the bureaucrats endeavoring to "get prices wrong," in Alice Amsden's wonderful phrase, instead of letting free markets get them right. There you have it: no capitalists, no Protestants, no merchants, no money, no market, no resources, not to mention no discernible history of commerce, foreign trade or industrial development, so on and so forth. And yet there it is.

Still Korea had comparative advantages. As early as 1888 an observant traveller, Percival Lowell, remarked of East Asian education that "if the peaks of intellect rise less eminent, the plateau of general elevation stands higher" than in the West. He was wrong about the "peaks," but right about the egalitarian belief, ultimately deriving from Confucian philosophy, in the inherent perfectibility of all humans. Thanks to a compulsory school system through the elementary level in the 1950s and 1960s, and later, middle and high school, the Korean work force was well-educated and better suited to industrial tasks than the workers of many other countries. The long tradition of bureaucratic governance by scholar-officials and an economy that reached pre-industrial peaks as high as anywhere else were excellent foundations for a state-led development program. Such people were also technocrats: their speciality was statecraft above all, but also agriculture, irrigation, hydraulic control of everything from rivers to lakes to reservoirs, military technology (armaments), even rockets (where, for example, the Chinese excelled). The state was the embodiment of knowledge. Why should not the state play a major role in the economy?

After Park's coup in 1961 the economy became a central part of the regime's planning focus and of its legitimacy. The state would be used to prime the economic pump and its success would be used to keep Park in power. By now South Korea could call upon a large cadre of economists and planners, many of whom had been trained in American universities; they shared a basic economic outlook with the multitude of American advisers in the economic aid mission, the embassy and institutions like the World Bank. New institutions like the Economic Planning Board (EPB) emerged to guide long-term plans (the first since the colonial period) for economic development.

With American support—and often pressure—the ROK in the early 1960s devalued its currency (making its exports much cheaper), provided state guarantees for businesses seeking foreign loans, gave tax holidays, exemptions or reductions to firms willing to produce for the export market, and developed plans for pushing export growth ahead at double-digit rates. Within a few years, exporting became a celebrated national pastime and patriotic activity, with Park blessing every new threshold of achievement.

American and Japanese firms were encouraged to relocate to Korea, where productivity was high and labor costs low. The typical industries were textile companies, light electronic manufactures like radios and calculators, and simple work and assembly processes such as stamping out nuts and bolts or glueing transistor boards. The foreign firms provided the requisite technologies and marketing know-how. Since textile and light electronic industries were in decline in both Japan and the United States, South Korea, with its disciplined labor force, was able to attract these industries and enable them to maintain their competitiveness in world markets. The gains for foreign firms were often remarkable. One Korean economist estimated that assembly workers in the Masan "Free Export Zone" were two and a half times as productive as American workers in the same industry, at one tenth the cost, yielding a 25-fold cost saving.

The role of the state in the South Korean economy is similar to that in Japan, with the Economic Planning Board performing the Japanese Ministry of International Trade and Industry (MITI) function. A major study of the Korean economy by a group of Harvard scholars concluded that "Korea, Inc." is a fairer characterization of the ROK's political economy than the "Japan, Inc." label is of Japan's: the state is chairman of the board, they say, with an even greater role in the economy than in Japan. Of particular importance is the credit function of the government. The regime is the broker for foreign loans, and thus is able to direct capital to productive, dynamic firms producing for export, and to penalize firms that are doing poorly. As Woo Jung-en has shown, this capital-provisioning function (often in the form of "policy loans") is a key element of the South Korean model of development, for it allows the state to select and foster firms that have comparative advantages in world markets.

The export-led program took off in the mid-1960s, in the period of the Second Five-Year Plan. According to some estimates, the ROK was for the next decade the most productive economy in the world, having an average annual industrial production growth rate of 25 percent and an incremental capital-output ratio (the amount of capital necessary to produce an additional unit of output) of 0.022, the lowest in the world. Its per capita gross national product (GNP) increased from $200 in 1960 to $800 by 1978, and the GNP itself went from $6 billion to $25 billion in the 1965–78 period. Exports were the major engine of this growth, increasing by 45 percent a year on the average in the early and mid-1970s. The leading sectors in this phase, however, were mostly light industries.

The Big Push

At his New Year's press conference in January 1973, Park announced a program of "heavy and chemical industrialization," with steel, autos, ships and machines projected to be 50 percent of 1980 export totals. The target was $10 billion in exports and $1000 per capita income within a decade. This was the press conference Park had wanted to give a decade earlier but could not; it was always his dream to make steel the symbol of his industrialization drive, not shoes or wigs. Steel meant national power, he often said; North Korea turned out thousands of tons of the stuff, an essential part of their armaments industry and just about everything else. The Pittsburgh of Korea was to be Pohang, a small port city nearly erased by the Korean War because of its location along the shifting lines of the Pusan Perimeter. Steel, however, was just one of six great industries to be built virtually overnight: the others were chemicals, automobiles, shipbuilding, machine tools and electronics.

Pohang Steel came onstream in 1973 with an annual capacity of 1 million tons; by 1976, 2.6 million tons of crude steel poured out of the mill, 5.5 million by 1978, 8.5 million by 1981. In a decade, South Korea's steel capacity grew 14-fold. Who bought all this steel? Korean shipbuilders who had no factories in 1970, Korean automakers who weren't supposed to be needed by the world market, American manufacturers who bought Korean steel delivered to the Midwest well below the posted price in Pittsburgh or Gary.

The export-led program ran aground in 1979, however, detonating political instability and leading to a 6 percent loss of GNP in 1980. Exports were expected to grow by 16 to 20 percent during 1979–82, but they were either stagnant or grew at 2 to 3 percent through the end of 1982. As the economy stalled, Korea's foreign debt grew to a total of $42 billion by early 1983 (Morgan Guaranty Trust Co. figures), the fourth largest in the world. The reasons for this crisis lay deep in the structure of Korea's economic activity. Exports met with ever higher protectionist barriers around the world. Technology transfers did not occur as expected, leaving Korea mainly with diminishing labor-cost advantages. Rapidly rising oil prices devastated an economy that had no oil of its own. The small domestic market could not make up for declining foreign markets, causing the auto industry and steel factories to run at 20 or 30 percent of capacity. Rising exports were needed to pay back foreign loans, and when exports fell the loans grew precipitously. Finally, the rapid growth of the economy had been unevenly distributed, causing grievances at home, particularly when expectations for ever greater growth were dashed in 1980.

After a profound shaking-out process in 1979–82, one which scared foreign investors and raised questions about the whole export-led program, the ROK got back on track by 1984. Unlike many Latin American nations, it did not experience problems in servicing its foreign debt. Exports began growing again in mid-1983 and topped $23 billion by year's end, a result in part of economic revival in the United States and general stability in oil prices. The economy then grew at an average annual rate of about 12 percent for three years running (1986–88), the highest rate in the world. The "Big Push," which had been the cause of the ROK's problems in the late 1970s, became the basis of rapid growth in the mid-1980s. South Korean planners thought they had entered another "crisis" in 1990 when the economy seemed to be growing at only a 7 percent rate—still among the highest in the world.

It was the Big Push that created Korea's big firms, now known by their names or logos all over the world. It is amazing to realize that this Korean business phenomenon is only as old as Park Chung Hee's early 1970s program: Daewoo did not exist until 1967, and the other big chaebol only went into heavy industry during this formative period or later. Nor was this a matter of technocrats doing market surveys and testing the waters: Park would call in the chaebol leaders and tell them what to do. At one point, so the story goes, Park heard that there was a big global demand for ocean-going tankers, mainly because of the Organization of Petroleum Exporting Countries shakeup in the global oil market, and the use of tankers for oil storage. He summoned Chung Ju Yung and exhorted him to start building ships. One big success piled on another, to the point where Korea rivaled Japan and the United States in high-tech electronics. By the mid-1980s, Korea became the third country in the world to manufacture 286-bit silicon wafers, and it filled the shelves of American discount houses with low-cost 286-chip home computers.

Irony of all ironies, 86 percent-dependent South Korea somehow yanked industrial self-reliance from the jaws of the world economy: after the Big Push, it had the basis to go all the way and develop a comprehensive industrial structure. It was a grand success, and a declaration of Korean independence. Ever since, Koreans have straightened their backs and walked with confidence; this is what still makes Park the most popular leader in postwar Korea (more than 70 percent of the population said so in a 1994 poll), in spite of his dictatorial ways. When the industrial sovereigns of the 20th century are lined up—Andrew Carnegie, Henry Ford, Joseph Stalin, Chairman Akio Morita of Sony—a Korean captain of industry will be among them.

Every last one of the chaebol was started by a family group, just like the Korean vegetable stores in New York City, and about 70 percent of them are still held by the founding family. A newspaper survey in 1989 reported that 60 percent of the founding-generation leaders of the top business groups own 80 percent or more of their companies' stocks. Like aristocracies elsewhere, the chaebol groups also intermarry at remarkable rates. According to one study, 31 out of the 33 largest firms have inter-chaebol marriages, and they often stay within the ranking (that is, the biggest marry the biggest, etc.). Samsung and Hyundai, for example, are linked by marriage alliances; often a chaebol-state alliance is also formed, as with Sunkyung (the chairman's son married Roh Tae Woo's daughter). In the mid-1990s, after much talk about scaling down the chaebols and diversifying the economy, the 10 largest still account for about 60 percent of all production, and the big four do 40 percent all by themselves. This means that 10 families control 60 percent of the "Miracle on the Han."

The Korean model of strong state-business coordination, huge concentration in the economy, government "policy loans" to dynamic firms and cheap labor cost advantages is still alive and well. In a recent German-Swiss survey of the comparative advantage of several industrial nations (three big ones, Japan, Germany, the United States, and three smaller ones, Italy, Spain, South Korea), Korea had the highest advantage, receiving a perfect score of 100 out of 100 on wage rates (whereas Japan was at 24 and the United States at 28) and 100 on tax burden or lack thereof (with Spain the next highest at 71, and the United States third at 55). In other words the Korean state still provided a relative capitalist heaven for the big-business groups. Company assets and the stock market have started to become more important sources of chaebol capital than state-mediated loans, although there are still many of the latter. The total value of the stock market increased 28-fold in the period 1980–89; that value was only 9 percent of Korea's GNP in 1985, but nearly 57 percent by 1988. In the early 1990s, it was the ninth-largest market in the world, and it is expected to be the fourth largest by the year 2000.

There is a darker side to this success. Independent labor unions still have questionable legitimacy (although labor organizing has been strong since 1987), and cheap labor continues to be Korea's main comparative advantage (the average hourly wage for factory workers in 1988 was $1.41, compared to $12.82 in the United States, $9.00 in Japan, and $2.50 in Singapore). The rural sector has not progressed rapidly and remains dependent on American grains. Big export firms have devastated the smaller firms producing for the national market. And, as argued earlier, Park and Chun combined the big role for the state in the economy with a strong role in governing, thinking that stability was necessary above all else. They thus laid waste Korean democracy.

The North Korean Economy

The DPRK has a socialist command economy with long-run plans (seven to ten years recently) and a bias toward heavy industry. It allows only a sharply limited role for market allocation, mainly in the rural sector where peasants sell produce from small private plots. In the last couple of years small numbers of private traders have appeared on city streets. Otherwise there is almost no small business.

Pyongyang has also sought a self-reliant, independent national economy; its claims of nearly complete self-reliance are discounted by foreign observers, but there is no question of its objective. Until the Soviet Union disappeared, it and China had provided petroleum, coking coal and advanced technology to North Korea, and had competed for influence with aid and technicians (now Russia and China compete to have economic relations with South Korea). North Korea has an energy regime that is only 10 percent dependent on imported petroleum (according to South Korean figures), which is a major achievement. The pursuit of self-reliance is, of course, primarily a matter of anti-imperial politics and foreign relations; it sacrifices efficiencies of scale and comparative advantage, but reflects the same desire in Pyongyang that animated Park Chung Hee, namely, to be "another Japan" with a fully developed industrial base.

In spite of coordinated central planning, the delivery of goods and services appears often to be decentralized to the neighborhood or village level, and several provinces are said to be self-reliant in food and consumer goods. Foreign visitors see few long lines in stores and restaurants, although resident diplomats say little is available in the shops.

For several decades the DPRK had one of the more successful socialist agricultural systems; CIA figures suggested that it was self-sufficient in food by the mid-1970s. Relying mostly on cooperative farms corresponding to the old natural villages rather than huge state farms, and using material incentives with little apparent ideological bias against them, the DPRK pushed agricultural production ahead rapidly. World Health Organization officials who visited in 1980 reported that "miracle" strains of rice were in wide use, and the U.S. CIA reported in a published study in 1978 that grain production had grown more rapidly in the North than in the South, that living standards in rural areas "have probably improved faster than in the South," and that "North Korean agriculture is quite highly mechanized, fertilizer application is probably among the highest in the world, and irrigation projects are extensive." In the 1980s the DPRK claimed to have the highest per hectare rice output in the world. Although that claim cannot be proved, experts did not question the North's general agricultural success, and published CIA figures put the DPRK's per capita grain output and fertilizer consumption among the highest in the world. By the 1990s, however, the combination of the collapse of North Korea's support from the former U.S.S.R., exports of grain for cash and several bad harvests led to many reports of food shortages, malnutrition and even starvation in the poorest rural areas of the DPRK. In 1993 the regime suggested that people eat two meals a day instead of three, which was an unprecedented admission of the difficulties the DPRK's food regime faced. Travelers to the cities, however, have not found bad conditions or much evidence of malnutrition. South Korea's rural population lives significantly better than that of the North, but North Korean peasants live better than their counterparts in many other countries of the world, and the regime has been very successful in health care, with nearly universal inoculation against various diseases. Life expectancy is at the level of second-rank industrial countries, and literacy is nearly universal, according to the UN.

Japanese Legacy: Heavy Industry

North Korea inherited a heavy industrial base from the Japanese era, and after several years of reorienting this base to serve Korean rather than Japanese needs, production grew rapidly. In the 1950s and 1960s annual average industrial growth rates were among the highest in the world, in the 25 to 30 percent range. Industrial growth slowed in the late 1960s as the "extensive" phase of expansion came to an end; plant depreciation and technological obsolescence took their toll; and transportation bottlenecks and fuel-resource problems also appeared and have plagued the economy ever since. In the early 1970s the DPRK sought to import new Western and Japanese technologies on a relatively large scale, buying whole plants on a binge basis. When world prices for some of the DPRK's mineral exports fell, the DPRK was unable to pay foreign creditors and defaulted on more than $1 billion in debts. In the 1980s, however, many of the creditors were satisfied, and the economy seems to have returned to reasonably good growth rates (the DPRK publishes few statistics, and most of those are percentages of previous production).

The 1978 CIA study estimated that the GNP of the DPRK stood at about $l0 billion in 1976, roughly half that of the ROK, giving both regimes roughly equivalent per capita GNPs. This probably held true through the South's recession in the early 1980s. Since 1983, however, the South has moved rapidly ahead in per capita terms. In 1979 Kim Il Sung claimed a per capita income of $l,900, and recently the DPRK put the figure at more than $2,500; but it is not known if the figure is accurate, or how it was arrived at. Published CIA figures place North Korea at around $1,000 in per capita GNP in the 1990s; U.S. and South Korean sources think the GNP slipped by 2 to 5 percent each year from 1991 through 1993, but that the economy began turning upward again in early 1994, if modestly. This is not good news for the DPRK, but neither do the figures signal a general crisis in the economy; after all, several post-Communist countries including Russia have lost 25 to 50 percent of GNP in the 1990s.

GNP figures do not give much indication of the quality of the DPRK's output, however. Although the quality cannot compare with South Korea's, the North does not do badly in goods of the second industrial revolution: steel, chemicals, hydroelectric power, internal-combustion engines, locomotives, motorcycles and various sorts of machine-building items. Where it lags far behind is in the communication technologies of the third industrial revolution: electronics, computers, semiconductor chips. Here North Korea has no hope unless it follows the path of China and Vietnam, opening its doors to foreign investment. The North has tried to interest foreign investors in a special export zone that it is building with Chinese help in the northeast corner of the country, and in early 1995 several firms in Hong Kong, France and Japan announced investment agreements in the Najin-Sonbong zone. But this is just a beginning.

Until the 1970s DPRK foreign trade was almost wholly with the Communist bloc, but in the past two decades imports and exports with Japan, Western Europe and various Third World nations have increased. By the mid-1970s, 40 percent of its trade was with non-Communist countries, and within the bloc only half was with the U.S.S.R.; but by the late 1980s, foreign exchange and other difficulties had left North Korea once again rather dependent on trade with the Soviet Union, and when the U.S.S.R. collapsed, along with other Communist countries in Eastern Europe, the loss of those markets for

North Korean goods caused great difficulty. Exporting has been a priority for several years, although the North in no sense has an export-led economy like the South. The focus on exports is to garner foreign exchange to import advanced technologies needed for further industrial growth and to pay for imported oil. The North Korean exporting policy has not been particularly successful to date, except perhaps in Japan. Its textile exports have been moderately successful, particularly among pro-DPRK residents in Japan.

In spite of these difficulties, American visitors to the DPRK in the 1980s and 1990s were often surprised by what they found. The rice fields are deep green and every inch of land is carefully tended; construction projects can be seen humming with round-the-clock shifts, contrary to South Korean reports that industry is at a standstill; people bustle through the streets to work at all hours; the cities suggest a clean, sparsely populated, diligent and efficient system. The countryside has an isolated, antiquarian, even bucolic atmosphere—reminiscent of the 1950s. Few families own TV sets or other consumer durables. At the same time there are no signs of the abject poverty and social pathology of all too many Third World countries. The majority of people are well-fed and plainly dressed, with little access to consumer goods. The elite drive around in Mercedes and Volvos in the cities and look like worldly professionals, which probably provokes resentment among the general populace.

North Faces Immense Challenge

Even on its own terms, the North faces a set of structural and seemingly irremediable problems unless it undertakes a major reform of the system. Its ponderous bureaucracy is impenetrable and exasperating to foreign businessmen; communications must go all the way to the top to get a decision within bureaucracies, and horizontal cooperation among bureaucracies is often nonexistent. The North's dogged desire for self-reliance has alienated the Russians and the Chinese and placed many obstacles in the way of trade with the West, not least being the lack of foreign exchange. Technological obsolescence means the North must import newer technologies if it hopes to compete with the South, but it is only beginning to adopt the new policies necessary to gain access to such technology (like changes in currency, new tax and profit laws for foreigners, space for market mechanisms), in contrast to China and Vietnam. Political rigidity has carried over into economic exchange; the North failed where the South succeeded in buying big steel mills from Japan, and thus the South leapt ahead of the North in steel production, which was always the North's forte.

Perhaps the most important change that Pyongyang has made in the mid-1990s is to try to cultivate better relations with the United States. As long as the DPRK maintained its stark hostility toward the United States with its forces against the South, it was never going to get the trade and technology that it claims to want and certainly needs. Perhaps now, with a new U.S.-DPRK relationship, it will.

On balance, and in spite of the DPRK's recent difficulties, the stress should be on the comparative economic successes of both Koreas. In the postwar period, both have been models of postcolonial development, if on entirely opposite systems and at different times. This means that a unified Korea would be a formidable industrial economy. How to account for this? Perhaps by remembering the stress on education in both systems, strong backing from big-power allies, effective use of state intervention in promoting economic development, and above all by keeping in mind the simple fact that neither are "new" states, but have grown out of an ancient and proud nation that began its modernization a century ago, not just in the postwar period.

7

Korea's Relationship to the World

MORE THAN 40 YEARS AFTER the end of the Korean War, the two Koreas still face each other across a bleak demilitarized zone (DMZ), engaged most of the time in unremitting, withering, unregenerate hostility, punctuated by occasional brief thaws and a few North-South exchanges. Huge armies are still poised to fight at a moment's notice. The Korean War solved nothing, but it did solidify armed bulwarks of containment, which the United States, the ROK, and the DPRK remain committed to, even in the post-cold-war world of the 1990s. Both Koreas continue to be deeply deformed by the necessity to maintain this unrelenting struggle. Yet around the peninsula so much has changed.

For a quarter century after 1945 the peninsula's position in a world-ranging conflict shaped the big powers' strategic logic. This small nation moved from a peripheral to a central role in the cold war because its hot war began at the point where two blocs intersected. The United States and 21 allied nations fought on the side of the South; China fought with the North and was backed by the U.S.S.R. and its allies. North Korea sought to roll back the South and the United States sought to roll back the North, and the failure of both in 1950 froze a global conflict at the DMZ, where it remains today.

For many years there was little momentum to alter the situation. In the 1960s some statesmen suggested major changes in American policy, among them Senator Mike Mansfield (D-Mont.) who called for Korea's demilitarization and neutralization. The ROK began actively to support American foreign policy, particularly with its dispatch of troops to fight in the Vietnam War (eventually more than 300,000 South Korean soldiers served there). The DPRK's position ranged from offering new unification policies (such as its call for a confederation in 1960) to committing hostile acts along the DMZ and against the United States (such as the seizure of the spy ship *Pueblo* in 1968).

Watershed changes in world politics by the 1970s seemed to deprive the cold-war logic of its meaning. With the emergence of the Sino-Soviet conflict, North Korea lost its joint backing and instead got a small war between the big Communist powers just across its border along the Ussuri River in 1969. With the Nixon opening to China in 1972, both North and South Korea watched helplessly as their great-power benefactors cozied up to each other and changed the calculus of strategy. Would the United States or China again intervene in a war in Korea if that intervention would destroy the new Sino-American relationship? Given the overriding importance of the gains both powers made by virtue of their new-found friendship, many thought the answer had to be no. With the ending of the Vietnam War in 1975, there were even fewer obstacles to ending the cold war throughout Asia.

The new strategic logic of the 1970s had an immediate and beneficial impact on Korea. The Nixon Administration withdrew a division of American soldiers without heightening tension; instead the North Koreans responded by virtually halting attempts at infiltration (compared to 1968 when more than 100 soldiers died along the DMZ) and by significantly reducing their defense budget in 1971. In what seemed to be a miraculous development, both Koreas held talks at a high level (between the director of the KCIA and Kim Il Sung's younger brother) in early 1972, culminating in a stunning July 4, 1972, announcement that both would seek reunification peacefully, independently of outside forces, and with common efforts toward creating a "great national unity" that would transcend the many differences between the two systems. Within a year that initiative had effectively failed, but it is a reminder of what might be accomplished through enlightened and magnanimous diplomacy and of the continuing importance of the unification issue.

The disorders in South Korea in 1979–80 and the emergence of the "new cold war" on a world scale froze the Korean situation for much of the 1980s. The Carter Administration dropped its program of troop withdrawal in 1979. The Reagan Administration, as its first foreign policy act, invited Chun Doo Hwan to visit Washington with the intention of bolstering ROK stability. The United States committed itself to a modest but significant buildup of men and equipment in South Korea. In the early 1980s some 4,000 American personnel were added to the 40,000 already there, advanced F-16 fighters were sold to Seoul, and huge military exercises ("Team Spirit") involving upward of 200,000 American and Korean troops were held toward the beginning of each year. Sino-American relations warmed considerably in 1983, and for the first time China said publicly that it wished to play a role in reducing tension in Korea. This was followed by a major DPRK initiative in January 1984 that called for the first time for three-way talks between the United States, the ROK and the DPRK. Previous to this, the DPRK had never been willing to sit down with both at the same time. (The Carter Administration had made a similar proposal for three-way talks in 1979.) The United States to date has not returned to this idea, however.

Beijing's Policy Shift

Through most of the 1980s Beijing sought to bring about talks between Washington and Pyongyang (talks which occasionally took place in Beijing between low-level diplomats) and encouraged Kim Il Sung to take the path of diplomacy. Chinese economic policy also shifted dramatically. By the end of the 1980s China had much more trade with South Korea than with North Korea, with freighters going back and forth directly across the Yellow Sea. Today South Korean firms are building factories or working with subsidiaries throughout the industrial regions of China.

The reemergence of détente in the mid-1980s and the ending of the cold war as the decade closed provided a major opportunity to resolve the continuing Korean confrontation. In particular, American-Soviet cooperation reduced tensions and Moscow took the initiative in opening diplomatic relations with the South. Since the collapse of the U.S.S.R., Moscow has isolated Pyongyang and has sought South Korean help with its economy.

South Korea has been effective in exploiting these new opportunities. In the late 1980s, it pursued an active diplomacy toward China, the Soviet Union and various East European countries, saying it would favor trade and diplomatic relations with "friendly" Communist regimes. This bore fruit in 1988 when most Communist countries attended the Seoul Olympics, with only Cuba honoring the North Korean "boycott." The collapse of East European communism grievously damaged North Korean diplomacy, as Hungary, Yugoslavia, Poland and other countries established diplomatic relations with Seoul. Today Seoul has good relations with all its former Communist enemies, many of whom look to it as a model of industrial development.

The two Koreas have made sporadic progress in relations with each other. The founder of the Hyundai conglomerate toured North Korea in January 1989 and announced a joint venture in tourism. The heads of other chaebol followed suit—especially Daewoo, which is developing a joint venture in the port of Nampo. By 1995 South Korean newspapers were filled with reports of business interest in the North, but relations between Seoul and Pyongyang were still sufficiently bad that much potential business activity between the two Koreas was still blocked.

Steps Toward Reconciliation

On December 13, 1991, the prime ministers of the ROK and the DPRK signed another "epochal" agreement on reconciliation, non-aggression, exchanges and cooperation in Seoul. Its 25 articles called for mutual recognition of the respective political systems, an end to mutual vilification and confrontation, "concerted efforts" to turn the Korean War armistice into a durable peace, guarantees of nonaggression, economic cooperation and exchange in many fields, and unrestricted travel through both halves of the country for the estimated 10 million Koreans separated from families by the war. Both sides also signed an agreement pledging to make the Korean peninsula nuclear-free. Soon even Reverend Sun Myung Moon, a fervent anti-Communist who had fled North Korea 40 years ago, showed up in North Korea to meet his relatives and hold talks with Kim Il Sung. As in the case of the 1972 agreements, however, most of the provisions of the 1991 pact have not been implemented.

The United States dragged its feet on Korea policy until the fall of 1991, allowing the other big powers to take the initiative. Then the Bush Administration abruptly announced it would withdraw all American nuclear weapons from Korea, raised the possibility that huge U.S.-ROK military exercises scheduled for early 1992 might be postponed, and in January 1992 dramatically upgraded the low-level talks it had been holding desultorily with the DPRK in Beijing over the past few years. That same month, the U.S. under secretary of state for political affairs, Arnold Kanter, met at the UN with the DPRK's Kim Yong Sun, an influential official who directs international affairs for the ruling party. The reason for all this activity was growing concern about the North's nuclear program. The Clinton Administration continued high-level talks with the North while broadening them beyond the nuclear issue; but it was the DPRK's nuclear program that stalled relations until late 1994.

The DPRK obtained a small research reactor (probably four megawatts) from the U.S.S.R. in 1964 and placed it under International Atomic Energy Agency (IAEA) safeguards in 1977. It then built a 30-megawatt facility at Yongbyon on the model of a 1950s-era British gas-graphite reactor fueled by uranium and known as the "Calder Hall." This type of reactor is much better for making nuclear weapons than it is for generating electricity (although it can have that function as well) because it yields high-grade plutonium that can then be reprocessed into weapons-grade fuel. This reactor went into operation about 1987. Subsequently, in 1989, spy satellites picked up apparent evidence of another reactor, of 50- to 200-megawatt capacity, which U.S. sources said might become operative in 1992; as of mid-1994, when the facility was frozen, it had not yet been completed. American officials were for years divided on what they thought were the real goals of the DPRK and had very little hard information to go on. The new worries about North Korea mainly arose from post-Gulf War inspec-

Former U.S. President Jimmy Carter with DPRK President
Kim Il Sung in June 1994.

tions of Iraq, which taught them how much can be concealed from satellites. Unnamed American officials travelling to Korea with President George Bush in January 1992 told reporters that they would require "a mandate to roam North Korea's heavily guarded military sites at will" before they could be sure of DPRK capabilities; that clearly was something the North was not willing to grant.

From then until October 1994, U.S.-DPRK relations lurched back and forth from crisis to diplomatic breakthroughs to crisis with no resolution of the problem. In May 1994 Pyongyang forced President Bill Clinton's hand by shutting down its reactor for the first time since 1989, withdrawing some 8,000 fuel rods. This called Washington's bluff and left officials with no apparent room for maneuver; predictably this act also occasioned another irresponsible media blitz about a new Korean War, a feature of media commentary since 1991. In this case, however, the alarms were warranted, unbeknownst to the media. The United States and North Korea came much closer to war at this time than most people realize, but former President Jimmy Carter learned of the depth of the crisis from briefings by Clinton Administration officials; frightened by what he had heard, he decided to take matters into his own hands.

Carter flew off to Pyongyang and by a sleight of hand that depended on CNN's simultaneous transmission of his discussions with Kim Il Sung on a boat in the Taedong River (direct TV mediation that short-circuited the ongoing diplomacy), he broke the logjam. Clinton appeared in the White House press room and declared that he was no longer interested in history: if Pyongyang were to freeze its program (that is, leave the fuel rods in the cooling ponds), high-level talks would resume—which they did on July 8 in Geneva. That was what made possible the real breakthrough that was consummated in October 1994.

The October framework agreement promised Pyongyang that in return for freezing its graphite reactors and returning to full inspections under the 1968 Treaty on the Non-Proliferation of Nuclear Weapons, a consortium of nations (including the United States, Japan, South Korea and others) would supply light-water reactors to help solve the North's energy problems and long-term loans and credits to enable Pyongyang to purchase the new reactors, valued at about $4 billion. In the meantime, the United States would supply heating oil to tide the DPRK over its energy problems and would begin a step-by-step upgrading of diplomatic relations. As of this writing teams of diplomats have been in both capitals seeking appropriate facilities to set up liaison offices. (In early 1995 the North balked at accepting South Korean light-water reactors because of fears of dependency on the South, but high-level negotiations solved that problem by relabeling the reactors.) The framework agreement is predicated on mutual mistrust, and therefore both sides must verify compliance at each step toward completion of the agreement, which will not come until the early part of the next century. By that time, if all goes well, the United States and the DPRK should finally have established full diplomatic relations, and the North's nuclear-energy program should be in full compliance with the nonproliferation regime.

Shortly after Carter's salutary intervention, Kim Il Sung died and the world watched to see if the succession to power of his son went badly or well. By mid-1995 there was nothing to indicate an unstable transition, although Kim Jong Il had not taken up all of his father's posts and continued to be called *yongdoja* rather than by his father's title of *suryong* (both terms translate as "leader," but suryong is of higher rank). When the North signed the October 1994 agreement, it was said to be at Kim Jong Il's explicit instruction. Today the top leadership in Pyongyang is a collective one of elders united around the younger Kim.

In the mid-1990s none of the great powers sees profit in conflict on the Korean peninsula, none would like to be involved in a new war and all would like relations with both Koreas, so the fault lines of cold-war conflict no longer exist there. In this situation, the United States has finally moved toward a more equidistant policy between the two Koreas, trying to play the role of honest broker while retaining its alliance with the South. Continued American troop commitments at pre-1989 levels have underlined Washington's support of Seoul, but the United States no longer lets Seoul dictate the pace of engagement with the North.

In the view of this author, the beginning of wisdom is to recognize that the United States continues to bear the greatest responsibility for peace on the Korean peninsula and in many ways for failing to resolve the Korean conflict nearly 50 years after it began. Nowhere else in the world has the United States backed one side of a conflict so exclusively, with such minimal contact with the other side. Nowhere else does the United States directly command the military forces of another sovereign nation, as it continues to do in South Korea.

Therefore it would be appropriate for the United States to take the initiative by drawing down and eventually ending its troop commitment in South Korea (there is increasing support for withdrawal in Congress), by expanding talks and trade with the North while continuing to support the South, by encouraging China and Japan to move toward equidistance in their treatment of both Koreas, and by pursuing every diplomatic and political means of reducing the high levels of tension that still remain. The October 1994 agreement is the first instance since the Korean War in which diplomacy has solved any important problem in Korea and if it is sincerely implemented by all sides, it should yield a divided Korea that is at peace. It may also hold the promise of future moves toward a reunified Korea, something that ultimately rests with the Korean people themselves and their capacity for magnanimity and reconciliation.

Talking It Over

A Note for Students and Discussion Groups

This issue of the HEADLINE SERIES, like its predecessors, is published for every serious reader, specialized or not, who takes an interest in the subject. Many of our readers will be in classrooms, seminars or community discussion groups. Particularly with them in mind, we present below some discussion questions—suggested as a starting point only—and references for further reading.

Discussion Questions

The author suggests that a number of traditional legacies exist in contemporary Korea. What are some of them, and how might they influence political systems as different as those in South and North Korea?

What role did the family play in Confucian societies? Did this affect the government or international relations, and if so, how?

Korea has a remarkable ethnic, linguistic and historical unity. How has this affected nationalism? With such a background, why should Korea remain divided?

If Japan helped to develop the Korean economy, why should there be such enmity between Koreans and Japanese? How can an economy be both overdeveloped and underdeveloped?

What effects did the colonial period have on Korea after 1945? Did these effects make the American occupation easy or difficult?

How was it that Korea came to be divided in 1945? Could this outcome have been avoided?

The author describes the Korean War as a civil war. What are the reasons for this? What are the civil aspects of the war? What role did external powers play in the Korean War?

What effect did the Chinese involvement have in the Korean War? Is the North Korean–Chinese relationship new or can one see traditional aspects to it?

What would you cite as the major reasons for economic growth in the ROK? Is this a market-driven economy, or a state-driven economy? What is the difference?

What are some of the successes and failures in South Korea's democratization? What are the remaining impediments to full democratization?

Kim Il Sung was in power longer than any postwar leader. How do you account for this? What do you think the future holds for North Korea now that he has passed from the scene?

How would you describe North Korea's relations with the former Soviet Union and China? Which model, the Soviet or the Chinese, has had more influence on the DPRK? How would you describe the unique features of the DPRK when compared to China or Russia?

What is Juche? Is it a Marxist philosophy? What does it signify for Koreans at home and for Korea's position in the world?

How did American diplomacy help to resolve the North Korean nuclear problem in the 1990s?

Can you suggest a formula for the peaceful reunification of the two Koreas? What would be a good policy to end the deadlock on the peninsula? Who should play a role in lessening tensions in Korea? The Koreans themselves? The United States? Other great powers?

Annotated Reading List

Amsden, Alice, *Asia's Next Giant: South Korea and Late Industrialization*. New York, Oxford University Press, 1989. A fine study showing how South Korea developed by "getting prices wrong," that is, by not following the advice of American economists.

Baldwin, Frank, ed., *Without Parallel: The American-Korean Relationship Since 1945*. New York, Pantheon Books, 1974. Critical and insightful essays on a number of postwar issues, including the UN and Korea, the ROK economy, and the failure of democracy in South Korea.

Clough, Ralph, *Embattled Korea: The Rivalry for International Support*. Boulder, Colo., Westview Press, 1987. A good overview of postwar Korea and its relations with the United States.

Cumings, Bruce, *The Origins of the Korean War*, 2 vols. Princeton, N.J., Princeton University Press, 1981, 1990.

———, ed., *Child of Conflict: The Korean-American Relationship, 1943–1953*. Seattle, University of Washington Press, 1983.

Eckert, Carter J., *Offspring of Empire: The Koch'ang Kims and the Colonial Origins of Korean Capitalism, 1876–1945*. Seattle, University of Washington Press, 1991. A case study of Korea's first chaebol group, family-held textile firms during the colonial period.

Foot, Rosemary, *The Wrong War: American Policy and the Dimensions of the Korean Conflict, 1950–1953*. Ithaca, N.Y., Cornell University Press, 1985. One of the best studies of the Korean War.

Haboush, Jahyun Kim, *A Heritage of Kings: One Man's Monarchy in the Confucian World*. New York, Columbia University Press, 1988. The best single study of a Korean king and his failed attempt to have his son succeed him, a story with great relevance for contemporary North Korea.

Harrison, Selig, ed., *Dialogue with North Korea*. Washington, D.C., Carnegie Endowment for International Peace, 1989. Dialogue between various American specialists and several North Koreans, covering the gamut of questions relating to Korea policy.

Hayes, Peter, *Pacific Powderkeg: American Nuclear Dilemmas in Korea*. New York, Free Press, 1990. The best study of nuclear problems in Korea after the Korean War.

Henderson, Gregory, *Korea: The Politics of the Vortex*. Cambridge, Mass., Harvard University Press, 1968. Excellent political history of Korea in modern times, combined with a theory of Korean society emphasizing centralization and a "vortex" process that is close to a mass-society theory.

Hicks, George, *The Comfort Women: Japan's Brutal Regime of Enforced Prostitution in the Second World War*. New York, W.W. Norton, 1995. The best study in English of this tragic episode in Korean-Japanese relations.

"The House that Park Built." *The Economist* (London), June 3, 1995. An 18-

page survey of South Korea's economy, politics and relations with the North.

Kim, Key-Hiuk, *The Last Phase of the East Asian World Order: Korea, Japan and the Chinese Empire, 1860–1882*. Berkeley, University of California Press, 1980. The best study of Korea's traditional foreign relations and the end of the Sinocentric world order.

Kuznets, Paul W., *Economic Growth and Structure in the Republic of Korea*. New Haven, Conn., Yale University Press, 1977. An excellent study of the South Korean economy's takeoff in the 1960s.

Lee, Chong-Sik, *The Politics of Korean Nationalism*. Berkeley, University of California Press, 1963. The standard political history of the subject.

Lee, Mun Woong, *Rural North Korea Under Communism: A Study of Sociocultural Change*. Houston, Tex., Rice University Special Studies, 1976. An excellent study of collectivized agriculture in North Korea.

Library of Congress, *North Korea: A Country Study*. 4th ed. Washington, D.C., U.S. Government Printing Office, 1994. An up-to-date study of North Korea, by several specialists.

Mason, Edward S., et al., *The Economic and Social Modernization of the Republic of Korea*. Cambridge, Mass., Harvard University Press, 1980. The summary volume of a major study of the South Korean economy.

Palais, James B., *Politics and Policy in Traditional Korea, 1864–1876*. Cambridge, Mass., Harvard University Press, 1976. By far the best study of the Yi Dynasty. The author has a thorough command of the extensive primary sources and provides a learned analysis of Korea's agrarian bureaucracy, the land system, the opening of Korea and many other subjects.

Scalapino, Robert, and Lee, Chong-Sik, *Communism in Korea. Vols. I & II: The Movement and The Society*. Berkeley, University of California Press, 1972. The most thorough treatment of North Korea.

Suh, Dae-Sook, *Korean Communism 1945–1980: A Reference Guide to the Political System*. Honolulu, The University of Hawaii Press, 1981.

———, *The Korean Communist Movement, 1918–1948*. Princeton, N.J., Princeton University Press, 1967. The first study to use the extensive collections of Japanese police reports on Korean communism, this is a standard work and comes with a companion volume of valuable documents.

Woo, Jung-en, *Race to the Swift: State and Finance in Korean Industrialization*. New York, Columbia University Press, 1991. The best analysis of the South Korean political economy.